COME TO THE CROSS

MW00998910

Inspired by God

Penned by
Matthew G. Morton

ISBN 979-8-88851-112-1 (Paperback)
ISBN 979-8-88851-113-8 (Digital)

Copyright © 2023 Matthew G. Morton
All rights reserved
First Edition

All rights reserved. No part of this publication may be reproduced, distributed, or transmitted in any form or by any means, including photocopying, recording, or other electronic or mechanical methods without the prior written permission of the publisher. For permission requests, solicit the publisher via the address below.

Covenant Books
11661 Hwy 707
Murrells Inlet, SC 29576
www.covenantbooks.com

CONTENTS

INTRODUCTION

About a year ago, God told me to write a book that would explain some of the hard-to-understand parts of the Bible for new believers. My first thought was, *God, you must have the wrong person.* Writing a book was one thing that had never crossed my mind. Then I thought about Moses at the burning bush and how he made excuses for why he could not do what God commanded him to do. I reluctantly decided to try.

After some time for prayer and trying to figure out where to begin, I came up with a plan. I was going to call the book "Ten Things New Christians Need to Understand about the Bible". The first chapter was going to be "Who Is God?". I sat at my computer for an hour or so thinking, but nothing was happening. I could not answer the question "Who is God?". The book went to the back burner, so to speak. This was in the summer of 2021.

August came, and I began my first year of classes at Bible College. In the fall semester, I took a theology class called the Doctrine of God the Trinity. When I had finished the course, I remembered the book and realized that I could then answer the question "Who is God?".

In early June, I began writing. I thought it would take me a couple of weeks to complete this project. It's now late September, and I'm still at it. I have now realized that the reason I couldn't write before is that I was trying to do it on my own—without God's help. That was a mistake. I learned to pray for God's inspiration before I pushed the power button.

One thing I want you to keep in mind while you are reading this book is that these words are all God inspired. There is no way I could have written this without His inspiration. I find it odd that the introduction is the last part of the book to be written. Also know that the devil did not want this book written; he fought me every day. The many distractions, headaches, and the nightmares were an obvious deterrent.

The book evolved as it was written, from a book intended for new believers into a book on salvation, for the whole world to read. *Come to the Cross* is a book about the incomprehensible love of God for all mankind. I take no credit nor criticism for what is written in these pages; this is all God. I'm just the guy holding the pen.

In the beginning God created the heavens and the earth.
—Genesis 1:1 NKJV

In the beginning was the Word, and the Word was with God, and the Word was God. He was in the beginning with God. All things were made through Him, and without Him nothing was made that was made. In Him was life, and the life was the light of men. And the light shines in the darkness, and the darkness did not comprehend it.
—John 1:1–5 NKJV

WHO IS GOD?

The Holy Trinity

If someone were to ask you who God is, what would your response be? What image comes into your mind as you think about God? When I was young, I would envision a black-and-white picture of an old man with a long white beard seated on a tall white throne with a scowling look on His face. Now, after years of Bible study and a close relationship with Him, I see something very different. Today I see an image of my Lord and Savior nailed to a Roman cross covered in blood. You might say to yourself, "That was Jesus, not God". Well, that leads us back to the question, Who is God?

Instead of asking who God is, maybe we should be asking, Who are they? This can be confusing, so read carefully. First we must realize that the word *God* is both singular and plural. God is a trinity. There are three divine spirits, or supernatural beings, that work together in a union that form one—the Almighty God.

> *For there are three that bear record in heaven, the Father, the Word, and the Holy Ghost: and these three are one. (1 John 5:7 KJV)*

The apostle John often refers to the Son of God as the Word in his writings.

God the Father, God the Son, and God the Holy Ghost or Holy Spirit are the three divine individuals that exist in concert and form the Holy Trinity of God. This is the correct view, or doctrine, of the orthodox Christian faith, which I believe wholeheartedly!

There are, however, certain religious groups that do not share this same view of the Trinity. The Jehovah's Witnesses, Christian Science, and the Mormon Church all have their own beliefs that I don't want to get into in this book. The United Pentecostals believe that there is one God that fills the three roles of the Father, Son, and Holy Ghost. One God, three roles. This theory is called *oneness* and not the correct view of the doctrine of the Trinity. This view, in my opinion, denies the deity of Christ and the Holy Spirit. Why would Jesus, the Son, pray to His Father if He was His Father? This theory makes no sense.

> *And he went a little further, and fell on his face, and prayed, saying,* ***"O my Father, if it be possible, let this cup pass from me: nevertheless, not as I will, but as thou wilt."*** *(Matthew 26:39 KJV)*

Jesus was in the garden at Gethsemane praying to His Father in heaven the night before His crucifixion.

Each of the three personalities of the Trinity, or Godhead, have their own identity and roles. We can see the members working together in these scriptures:

> *The God of our fathers raised up Jesus whom you murdered by hanging on a tree. Him hath God has exalted with His right hand to be a Prince and Savior, for to give repentance to Israel and forgiveness of sins. And we are His witnesses to these things, and so is also the Holy Ghost whom God hath given to them who obey Him. (Acts 5:30–32 NKJV)*

How God anointed Jesus of Nazareth with the Holy Spirit and with power, who went about doing good and healing all who were oppressed by the devil, for God was with Him. (Acts 10:38 NKJV)

For there is one God and one Mediator between God and men, the Man Christ Jesus. (1 Timothy 2:5 NKJV)

But when the helper comes, whom I shall send to you from the Father, the Spirit of truth who proceeds from the Father, He will testify of Me. (John 15:26 NKJV)

The Three also communicate or speak to each another.

Then God said, "Let Us make man in Our image, according to Our likeness; let them have dominion over the fish of the sea, over the birds of the air, and over the cattle, over all the earth and over every creeping thing that creeps on the earth." (Genesis 1:26 NKJV)

Then the Lord God said, "Behold, the man has become like one of Us, to know good and evil. And now, lest he put out his hand and take also of the tree of life, and eat, and live forever." (Genesis 3:22 NKJV)

In some scriptures, it can be difficult to determine which of the Three God is referring to. In Hebrews 1, God the Father is exalting the Son by acknowledging that He (the Son) is God.

For to which of the angels did He ever say: "You are My Son, today I have begotten You"?

> *And again: "I will be to Him a Father, And to Me He shall be a Son"? But when He again brings the first-Born into the world, He says: "Let all of the angels of God worship Him." And of the angels He says: "Who makes His angels spirits And His ministers a flame of fire." But to the Son He says: "Your throne, O God is forever and ever; A scepter of righteousness is the Scepter of Your kingdom. You have loved righteousness and hated lawlessness; Therefore God, Your God, has Anointed You With the oil of gladness more than Your companions." (Hebrews 1:5–9 NKJV)*

Just for the sake of understanding, let's compare the Trinity to a music group, a trio. One member sings bass, one is a tenor, and the third, an alto. Let's call them the One. They each play multiple instruments. They can perform together in one location or separately. But when they perform, it is glorious! Three performers make up the One. Each member complements the others in perfect harmony. Of course, this is an oversimplification of the Trinity of God. No human mind can remotely comprehend the greatness of the Almighty God.

THE ATTRIBUTES OF GOD

In this next segment, I want to tell you about God. I want you to understand His nature, His motives, His desires, and, more importantly, what God says about Himself in His Holy Word, the Bible.

> God is the supreme being, the creator and ruler of all that is; the self-existent one, who is perfect in power, goodness, and wisdom. (GotQuestions.org)

God the Creator

God (the Trinity) is the eternal creator of everything.

> *In the beginning God created the heaven and the earth. (Genesis 1:1 KJV)*

Let's examine Genesis 1:1: "In the beginning [time] God [the Trinity] created [designed and manufactured from nothing] the heaven [space] and the earth [matter]."

God created time, space, and matter. Before God created time, time did not exist. Before God created space, space did not exist. Before God created matter, matter did not exist. Therefore, or however, God is not bound by time, space, or matter; He rules over them. God has always existed and will always exist.

If we as human beings can understand and fully accept the truth of Genesis 1:1, we can surely accept the entirety of the Bible.

For those who cannot accept this verse, the Bible will have little relevance.

> *For by Him were all things created that are in heaven and that are in earth, visible and invisible, whether they be thrones or dominions, or principalities or powers. All things were created through Him, and for Him. And He is before all things, and in Him all things consist. (Colossians 1:16–17 NKJV)*

> *You are worthy, O Lord, to receive glory and honor and power; For You created all things, And by Your will they exist and were created. (Revelation 4:11 NKJV)*

God is holy

Holy means "exalted or worthy of complete devotion as one perfect in goodness and righteousness" (*Merriam-Webster Dictionary*).

Author's definition, to be free or separate from sin and unrighteousness.

God hates sin! God cannot sin; that would be contrary to His holy nature. He won't even be around sin. Christ Jesus had to shed His blood to cover the sins of man so that the Holy God could have a relationship with mankind.

> *Speak to all the congregation of the children Israel, and say to them: You shall be holy, for I the Lord your God am holy. (Leviticus 19:2 NKJV)*

> *Exalt the Lord our God, and worship at His holy hill; For the Lord our God is holy. (Psalms 99:9 NKJV)*

God is omnipotent

God is omnipotent, or all-powerful. God possesses the infinite power to create and maintain the universe. Think about how much energy is in the sun. Scientists have determined that there are approximately two hundred sextillion stars in the universe. That is 200,0 00,000,000,000,000,000,000! That is mind boggling. Our sun is considered an average-sized star. Every second, "the sun produces the same energy as a trillion 1 megaton bombs!" (*The Boston Globe*, September 5, 2005). Now think about that power multiplied by two hundred sextillion. That is infinite power. And God created and knows the name of each star.

> *Lift up your eyes on high, and see who has created these things, who brings out their host by number; He calls them all by name, By the greatness of His might and the strength of His power, not one is missing. (Isaiah 40:26 NKJV)*

> *He counts the number of the stars; He calls them all by name. Great is our Lord, and mighty in power. His understanding is infinite. (Psalm 147:4–5 NKJV)*

> *The heavens declare the glory of God; and the firmament shows His handiwork. (Psalm 19:1 NKJV)*

The awesome power of God displayed by His creation of all the stars is truly amazing, but that's just a sample of the omnipotence of the Almighty God. God has the ability and power to do whatever He pleases whenever and however He chooses.

> *Ah, Lord God! Behold, you have made the heavens and the earth by Your great power*

> *and outstretched arm. There is nothing too hard for You. You show lovingkindness to thousands and repay the iniquity of the fathers into the bosom of their children after them—the Great, the Mighty God, whose name is the LORD of hosts. (Jeremiah 32:17–18 NKJV)*

God is omniscient

God is omniscient, or all-knowing. He knows everything. Remember, God is not bound by time; He lives in the past, present, and future. God knows everything you have ever done. He knows all about you—every hair on your head. He knows every decision that you are going to make. It's amazing that He knows all and yet allows us to make our own decisions, good or bad. Even more amazing, He knows every detail about every person who has or will ever live. My guess is around five hundred billion souls have lived on earth; God knows the exact number at any given second. I truly believe that God planned the exact time of birth of every human and knows the exact time we will all breath our last breath. God knows all.

> *For there is not a word on my tongue, but behold, O Lord, you know it altogether. (Psalm 139:4 NKJV)*

> *Would not God search this out? For He knows the secrets of the heart. (Psalm 44:21 NKJV)*

> ***But the very hairs of your head are all numbered. (Matthew 10:30 NKJV)***

> *The Lord looks from heaven; He sees all the sons of men. From the place of His dwelling, He looks on all the inhabitants of the earth; He fashions their hearts individually;*

> *He considers all their works. (Psalm 33:13–15 NKJV)*

God is omnipresent

God is omnipresent, or everywhere. God is not bound by space or time. He exists in spirit, not physical form. He can be in your house, your heart, your head, and anywhere and everywhere all at the same time. God knows no limits.

> *"Am I a God near at hand," says the Lord, "And not a God far off? Can anyone hide himself in secret places, So I shall not see him?" says the Lord; "Do I not fill heaven and earth?" says the Lord. (Jeremiah 23:23–24 NKJV)*

> *Where can I go from your spirit? Or where can I flee from your presence? If I ascend into heaven, you are there; if I make my bed in hell, behold, you are there. If I take the wings of the morning, and dwell in the uttermost parts of the sea, ever there your hand shall lead me, and your right hand shall hold me. If I say, "Surely the darkness shall fall on me," Even the night shall be light about me; Indeed, the darkness shall not hide from you, But the night shines as the day, The darkness and the light are both alike to You. For you formed my inward parts, you covered me in my mother's womb. I will praise You, I will praise You, for I am fearfully and wonderfully made; Marvelous are Your works, and that my soul knows very well. My frame was not hidden from You, When I was made in secret, and skillfully wrought in*

> *the lowest parts of the earth. (Psalm 139:7–15 NKJV)*

God is love

God loves all He created. In Genesis chapter 1, we read, when God had finished His creation, He was well pleased.

> *Then God saw everything that He had made, and indeed it was very good. So, the evening and the morning were the sixth day. (Genesis 1:31 NKJV)*

During the sixth day of creation, God had created heaven and earth—everything in the heaven and everything on the earth. He had been preparing a dwelling place or home for His grand finale, mankind.

> *So, God created man in His own image; in the image of God, He created him; male and female He created them. Then God blessed them, and God said to them, "Be fruitful and multiply; fill the earth and subdue it; have dominion over the fish of the sea, over the birds of the air, and over every living thing that moves on the earth." And God said, "See, I have given you every herb that yields seed which is on the face of all the earth, and every tree whose fruit yields seed; to you it shall be for food. Also, to every beast of the earth, to every bird of the air, and to everything that creeps on the earth, in which there is life, I have given every green herb for food"; and it was so. (Genesis 1:27–30 NKJV)*

God created man and woman and gave them dominion over His creation. God said to them, "Be fruitful and multiply; fill the earth and subdue it". It is obvious that God cared more for the man and woman than the rest of His creation. In fact, all He created was for them. God gave everything to them because He loved them and wanted a relationship with them. God so loved them—Adam and his wife, Eve—that He put them in a beautiful garden to live.

In Genesis 3, we read that God was enjoying His relationship with Adam and his wife; then one day, something happened that would alter the relationship between God and mankind forever: they sinned. You know the story; they ate of the tree of knowledge of good and evil that God had forbidden them to eat. Now remember, God is omniscient. He knew this was going to happen. Also, remember that God cannot be involved with sin. So God had a plan to deal with their disobedience.

God confronted them about this sinful thing that they had done and cast them out of the garden. Now God still loved the man and woman, but this sin was a real problem and had to be dealt with. There is always a consequence for sin. Now this is very important. God loved them and wanted to repair and maintain His relationship with them. So He killed an animal, probably a lamb, and made clothes for them from the skin of the lamb. The blood of the sacrificed lamb covered their sin.

This disobedience, or sin, is known as the fall of man. And the blood sacrifice of an innocent lamb covering the sin of man is the first account of the Gospel in the Bible. We will come back to this again in this book. The point here is that God loves man so much that He will never turn away from him even though man has sinned against God.

> *Unto Adam also and to his wife did the Lord God make coats of skins, and clothed them. (Genesis 3:21 KJV)*

> *Yet hear now, O Jacob My servant, And Israel whom I have chosen. Thus says the* LORD

> *who made you and formed you from the womb, who will help you: "Fear not, O Jacob My servant; And you, Jeshurun, whom I have chosen. For I will pour water on him who is thirsty, and floods on the dry ground; I will pour My Spirit on your descendants, And My blessing on your offspring." (Isaiah 44:1–3 NKJV)*

> *They refused to obey, and they were not mindful of Your wonders That You did among them. But they hardened their necks, and in their rebellion, they appointed a leader to return to their bondage. But You are God, ready to pardon, gracious and merciful, slow to anger, abundant in kindness, and did not forsake them. (Nehemiah 9:17 NKJV)*

> *But You, O Lord, are a God full of compassion, and gracious, longsuffering and abundant in mercy and truth. (Psalms 86:15 NKJV)*

I could go on and on and never cover all the attributes of the true nature of God. Let's read a scripture where the Almighty is speaking about Himself.

> *Thus says the* LORD, *the King of Israel, and his Redeemer, the* LORD *of hosts: "I am the First and I am the Last; Besides Me there is no God. And who can proclaim as I do? Then let him declare it and set it for Me, Since I appointed the ancient people. And the things that are coming and shall come, let them show these to them. Do not fear, nor be afraid; Have I not told you from that time, and declared it? You are My witnesses. Is there a God besides*

> *Me? Indeed, there is no other Rock; I know not one." (Isaiah 44:6–8 NKJV)*

The attributes of God in summary

God is omnipotent (all-powerful; Jeremiah 32:17–18).
God is infinite (without limits; Romans 11:33).
God is good (kind and caring; Psalm 119:65–72).
God is love (sacrificed His Son for us; 1 John 4:7–10).
God is immutable (perfect and unchanging; Psalm 102:25–28).
God is transcendent (the highest being; Psalm 113:4–5).
God is just (always fair in His judgments; Psalm 75:1–7).
God is holy (perfect and above all sin; Revelation 4:8–11).
God is self-sufficient (man is dependent on God, but God needs nothing; Acts 17:24–28).
God is omniscient (all-knowing; Psalm 139:1–6).
God is omnipresent (always everywhere; Psalm 139:7–12).
God is merciful (compassionate toward man; Deuteronomy 4:29–31).
God is sovereign (rules over all creation; 1 Chronicles 29:11–13).
God is wise (perfect wisdom and knowledge; Proverbs 3:19–20).
God is faithful (honors His covenants; Psalm 89:1–8).
God is wrathful (judging and punishing to all evil; Nahum 1:2–8).
God gives grace (unmerited favor; Ephesians 1:5–8).
God is our comforter (believers are comforted knowing He is with us; 2 Corinthians 1:3–4).
God is Father (God is our eternal Father; Romans 8:15–17).

> An intelligent personal Spirit…infinite, eternal, unchangeable in His being, in His wisdom, in His holiness, and in all perfections consistent with His being. (A. A. Hodge)

I will conclude this segment with a quote from the great pastor and teacher Dr. John Yates:

> He is God, the one God, the only God, and the eternal God. He is personal, perfect, free, intelligent, sovereign, omnipotent, omniscient, and omnipresent. He is Spirit. He is love and light. He is the uncaused first caused of all things, the Self-sufficient Creator and Sustainer of all things, the Lawgiver, and the Judge. He is holy and just, gracious, and merciful. He is infinite and incomprehensible. He is immutable, perfect, glorious, and worthy of all worship and obedience. He is transcendent above His creation, but is actively involved in caring for His creation and Man. He is our Supplier, our Redeemer, and our Savior. He loves us and desires to know us. He is One God Who exists as three co-equal, co-eternal Persons. He is Father, Son, and Holy Ghost. He is God! (Dr. John Yates, Faith Bible Institute)

THE NAMES OF GOD

God has many names other than just God. Some theologians claim that there are more than one hundred names for God. However, most of those names are titles given by men. Let us examine some of these more common names and titles of God. There are three primary names of God in the Old Testament. These are personal names, like your name is personal to you. The other names of God are compounds, or forms, of the three primary names that reflect different attributes or characteristics of God.

Before we get started, I want to point out that the Old Testament books were originally written in the Hebrew language, with 267 verses written in Aramaic. These Aramaic verses are in the books of Ezra, Daniel, and Jeremiah; but will have no bearing on these names that we will study. If you are reading a Bible written in English, God's name may appear in English or Hebrew, so it is good to know the translation of each name. The primary names of God are Elohim, YHWH or Jehovah, and Adonai.

Elohim, translated "God," refers to God's infinite power in relation to the creation. *Elohim* is the plural of *Eloah*, which reflects the doctrine of the Trinity. The infinite power of God (Elohim) is exemplified in Genesis 1:1 as He speaks into existence the heaven and the earth:

> *In the beginning God created the heaven and the earth. (Genesis 1:1 KJV)*

The original Hebrew text would have the name *Elohim* in place of *God*:

> *In the beginning God (Elohim) created [by forming from nothing] the heavens and the earth. (Genesis 1:1 AMP)*

YHWH and **Jehovah** are the same name.

> *Yahweh* is the promised name of God. This name of God which (by Jewish tradition) is too holy to voice, is spelled "YHWH" without vowels. *YHWH* is referred to as the Tetragrammaton (which simply means "the four letters"). *YHWH* comes from the Hebrew letters: Yud, Hay, Vav, Hay. While *YHWH* is first used in Genesis 2, God did not reveal Himself as YHWH until Exodus 3. The modern spelling as "Yahweh" includes vowels to assist in pronunciation. Many pronounce *YHWH* as "Yahweh" or "Jehovah." We no longer know for certain the exact pronunciation. During the third century AD, the Jewish people stopped saying this name in fear of contravening the commandment *"Thou shalt not take the name of the LORD thy God in vain" (Exodus 20:7)*. As a result of this, *Adonai* is occasionally a substitute for *YHWH*. The following compound names which start with "YHWH" have been shown using "Jehovah." This is due to the common usage of "Jehovah" in the English of these compound names in the early English translations of the Bible (e.g., the Geneva Bible, the King James Version, etc.). (Don Stewart, Blue Letter Bible; emphasis added)

YHWH or *Jehovah*, "LORD" (all caps), means "I AM," as in "I am the LORD."

> *And God said unto Moses, I AM THAT I AM: and he said, thus shalt thou say unto the children of Israel, I AM hath sent me unto you. (Exodus 3:14 KJV)*

Adonai, "Lord God," was used as a substitute for *YHWH*, which the Hebrews would not speak or write.

> *Then David went in, sat before ADONAI and said, "Who am I, Adonai ELOHIM; and what is my family, that has caused you to bring me this far? Yet in your view, Adonai ELOHIM, even this was too small a thing; so you have even said that your servant's dynasty will continue on into the distant future. This is [indeed] a teaching for a man, Adonai ELOHIM—what more can David say to you? For you know your servant intimately, Adonai ELOHIM." (2 Samuel 7:18–20 CJB)*

Let's study some other names or titles of God:

- **El-Shaddai** (God Almighty)—This speaks of God's infinite power over all.

> *And when Abram was ninety years old and nine, the LORD appeared to Abram, and said unto him, I am the Almighty God; walk before me, and be thou perfect. (Genesis 17:1 KJV)*

> *When Abram was 99 years old ADONAI appeared to Avram and said to him, "I am El*

Shaddai [God Almighty]. Walk in my presence and be pure-hearted." (Genesis 17:1 CJB)

I appeared to Abraham, Isaac, and Jacob by the name God Almighty [El Shaddai], but they did not know me by my name, the Lord [Yahweh]. (Exodus 6:3 Expanded Bible)

- **El Elyon** (God Most High)—This denotes exaltation and speaks of God's absolute right to lordship.

I will cry out to God Most High, To God who performs all things for me. (Psalm 57:2 NKJV)

I call to Elohim Elyon, to El who does everything for me. (Psalm 57:2 Names of God Bible)

I will cry unto God most high; unto God that performed all things for me. (Psalm 57:2 KJV)

- **Jehovah Rapha** (the Lord who heals)—God heals both body and soul.

And said, "If you diligently heed the voice of the Lord your God and do what is right in His sight, give ear to His commandments and keep all His statutes, I will put none of the diseases on you which I have brought on the Egyptians. For I am the Lord who heals you." (Exodus 15:26 NKJV)

- **Jehovah Jireh** (the Lord will provide)—God provides for His people.

And Abraham called the name of that place Jehovah Jireh: as it is said to this day, In the mount of the LORD it shall be seen. (Genesis 22:14 KJV)

Therefore do not worry, saying, "What shall we eat?" or "What shall we drink?" or "What shall we wear?" For after all these things the Gentiles seek. For your heavenly Father knows that you need all these things. (Matthew 6:31–32 NKJV)

- **Jehovah Nissi** (God our banner)—God is our source for victory through our trials and battles.

And Moses built an altar, and called the name of it Jehovah Nissi. (Exodus 17:15 KJV)

- **Jehovah Rohi or Raah** (the Lord my shepherd)—The Lord leads and protects us from danger.

The LORD is my shepherd; I shall not want. He maketh me to lie down in green pastures: he leadeth me beside the still waters. He restoreth my soul: he leadeth me in the paths of righteousness for his name's sake. Yea, though I walk through the valley of the shadow of death, I will fear no evil: for thou art with me; thy rod and thy staff they comfort me. Thou preparest a table before me in the presence of mine enemies: thou anointest my head with oil; my cup runneth over. Surely goodness and mercy shall follow me all the days of my life:

and I will dwell in the house of the LORD forever. (Psalm 23:1–6 KJV)

- **Jehovah Shammah** (the Lord is there)—This name is found in the book of Ezekiel. During the time when the Israelites were in captivity in Babylon (the exile) and Jerusalem and the Holy Temple lay in ruins, God appeared to Ezekiel in a vision and revealed to him that His people, Jerusalem, and the temple would all be restored to greatness. In the last verse of Ezekiel, God declares that the city will be called "the Lord Is There" (Jehovah Shammah).

It was round about eighteen thousand measures: and the name of the city from that day shall be, The LORD is there. (Ezekiel 48:35 KJV)

- **Jehovah Tsidkenu** (the Lord our righteousness)—This name is found in the book of Jeremiah. During the exile of Judea, God raised up profits to speak to His people, telling them that if they (God's people) would repent and return to Him, He would restore them, therefore becoming their righteousness. *Tsidkenu* means "righteousness."

Behold, the days come, saith the LORD, that I will raise unto David a righteous Branch, and a King shall reign and prosper, and shall execute judgment and justice in the earth. In his days Judah shall be saved, and Israel shall dwell safely: and this is his name whereby he shall be called, THE LORD OUR RIGHTEOUSNESS. (Jeremiah 23:5–6 KJV)

- **Jehovah Mekoddishkem** (the Lord who sanctifies)—This name reflects that God is the one who sanctified His people Israel, made them holy, and set them apart to His own.

  Sanctify yourselves therefore and be ye holy: for I am the Lord your God. And ye shall keep my statutes and do them: I am the Lord which sanctify you. (Leviticus 20:7–8 KJV)

- **Jehovah Shalom** (the Lord is peace)—This name comes from the book of Judges. After Gideon had led his small army to victory over the Midianites, God had given the Israelites peace. God wants us to know peace through Him.

  Then Gideon built an altar there unto the Lord and called it Jehovah Shalom: unto this day it is yet in Ophrah of the Abiezrites. (Judges 6:24 KJV)

- **Jehovah Sabaoth** (the Lord of hosts)—This name reflects God's reign over heaven and earth and over all armies, earthly and spiritual. *Sabaoth* is a Hebrew word that means "that which goes forth."

  Then said David to the Philistine, Thou comest to me with a sword, and with a spear, and with a shield: but I come to thee in the name of the Lord of hosts, the God of the armies of Israel, whom thou hast defied. (1 Samuel 17:45 KJV)

  Praise ye him, all his angels: praise ye him, all his hosts. (Psalm 148:2 KJV)

- **El Roi** (the God that sees me)—God sees the needs, the hurts, the heart, and the sins of all His people.

> *And she called the name of the LORD that spake unto her, Thou God seest me: for she said, Have I also here looked after him that seeth me? (Genesis 16:13 KJV)*

> *But the LORD said unto Samuel, look not on his countenance, or on the height of his stature; because I have refused him: for the LORD seeth not as man seeth; for man looketh on the outward appearance, but the LORD looketh on the heart. (1 Samuel 16:7 KJV)*

GOD'S PERFECT PLAN

Before God created the heaven and the earth, God alone was all that existed—just the Father, the Son, and the Holy Spirit and nothing else as far as we know. Can you imagine what that would be like to be the only *one*, with nothing else?

I believe that it would be very lonely, but God had a plan, a brilliant plan that would inevitably give Him a family—a large family of people created in His image that would, willingly and through free will, choose to love and exalt Him over themselves. God could have created man to do whatever He ordered him to do without question, like robots, but God gave man free will to make his own decisions and choices. This free will left man vulnerable to temptation, his own desires, and disobedience to God.

In Genesis 3, we read about mankind's first account of temptation and sin against God, when Adam and his wife ate of the forbidden tree. This disobedience not only cost Adam and Eve their comfortable life in the garden but they would be cursed and forced to work hard for their food and shelter (Genesis 3:16–19,23–24). This sin, the fall of man, eventually cost them their lives. Adam lived 930 years, and he died (Genesis 5:5). Based on the Scriptures, I believe that God originally intended for man to not know death. Man sinned against God, and the ramification was eventual death (Genesis 1:26–27; Genesis 2:17; Romans 5:12).

In the next chapter, Genesis 4, we read about man's first murder, where Adam's son Cain kills his brother, Abel, out of jealousy (Genesis 4:8). By the time we get to Genesis 6, the world had gotten so sinful and corrupt that God brought a great flood that destroyed all the people except one man, Noah, and his family (Genesis 6:5–8). You probably know the story of Noah and the ark.

At this point, it looks like God had made a huge mistake by giving man free will, but remember that God is omniscient and makes no mistakes. This all had to come to pass to fulfill God's eternal plan. God did not want nor cause man to sin; God gave man the free will to make his own decisions. Even today, people ask why God allows all the violence in the world to go on. The answer is free will. God knows that no man nor woman can live without ever committing sin. So God sent His Son in the flesh of a man to teach mankind how He wanted us to live, how to worship Him, and how to be saved from our sins.

This man, Yeshua (Jesus), was quite unique. He was born from a virgin woman. His Father was through the Holy Spirit, and therefore, He had no sin nature and never committed a single sin. He was completely human and fully God. He walked with man thirty-three years before He was crucified on a Roman cross. Do you remember in Genesis 3 when God killed the innocent lamb to cover the sin of Adam and Eve? Well, Jesus, the Son of God, the only sinless man to ever live, had to die and shed His perfect blood as a sacrifice to cover the sins of all mankind so man would not have to die for his sins.

> ***For God so loved the world, that he gave his only begotten Son, that whosoever believeth in him should not perish, but have everlasting life. (John 3:16 KJV)***

These are the greatest words I've ever heard! This is known as the Gospel of Jesus Christ. The Son of God, Jesus Christ, died a terrible, painful death on a Roman cross for you and me and everyone who will ever live so that we can be pardoned of our sins and be accepted by Almighty God and live with Him in His kingdom forever. Amen! It is God's desire for every man, woman, and child to accept salvation from sin and live forever with Him. But many will choose to reject the Gospel of salvation and will die. For those who will reject the Gospel, they will be condemned to another place, separated from the glory of God. And for them, there will be great pain and gnashing of teeth.

> *And shall cast them into the furnace of fire: there shall be wailing and gnashing of teeth. (Matthew 13:50 KJV)*

> *Who shall be punished with everlasting destruction from the presence of the Lord, and from the glory of his power. (2 Thessalonians 1:9 KJV)*

The good news is that Jesus rose from the dead and returned to be with His Father, but He shall return soon to gather His people and take us unto His kingdom. For everyone who can understand and accept the salvation that Jesus died for shall be saved and live with God forever.

> *There is therefore now no condemnation to them which are in Christ Jesus, who walk not after the flesh, but after the Spirit. (Romans 8:1 KJV)*

> *Jesus said to him,* ***"I am the way, the truth, and the life. No one comes to the father except through Me."*** *(John 14:6 NKJV)*

> *That if you confess with your mouth the Lord Jesus and believe in your heart that God has raised Him from the dead, you will be saved. For with the heart one believes unto righteousness, and with the mouth confession is made unto salvation. (Romans 10:9–10 NKJV)*

This is God's plan to have His family, that all people that choose Him through free will and the blood of Jesus Christ shall dwell in the house of the Lord forever. Amen.

THE HISTORY OF MAN'S SIN

Let's go back to Genesis 3:

> *Now the serpent was more cunning than any beast of the field which the* L*ORD* *God had made. And he said to the woman, "Has God indeed said, 'You shall not eat of every tree of the garden'?"*
>
> *And the woman said to the serpent, "We may eat the fruit of the trees of the garden; but of the fruit of the tree, which is in the midst of the garden, God has said, 'You shall not eat it, nor shall you touch it, lest you die.'"*
>
> *Then the serpent said to the woman, "You will not surely die. For God knows that in the day you eat of it your eyes will be opened, and you will be like God, knowing good and evil."*
>
> *So, when the woman saw that the tree was good for food, that it was pleasant to the eyes, and a tree desirable to make one wise, she took of its fruit and ate. She also gave to her husband with her, and he ate. Then the eyes of both were opened, and they knew that they were naked; and they sewed fig leaves together and made themselves coverings.*
>
> *And they heard the* L*ORD* *God walking in the garden in the cool of the day, and Adam and his wife hid themselves from the presence of the* L*ORD* *God among the trees of the garden.*

Then the LORD God called to Adam and said to him, "Where are you?"

So, he said, "I heard Your voice in the garden, and I was afraid because I was naked; and I hid myself."

And He said, "Who told you that you were naked? Have you eaten from the tree of which I commanded you that you should not eat?"

Then the man said, "The woman whom You gave to be with me, she gave me of the tree, and I ate."

And the LORD God said to the woman, "What is this you have done?"

The woman said, "The serpent deceived me, and I ate."

So, the LORD God said to the serpent: "Because you have done this, you are cursed more than all cattle, and more than every beast of the field; On your belly you shall go, and you shall eat dust all the days of your life. And I will put enmity between you and the woman, and between your seed and her Seed; he shall bruise your head, and you shall bruise His heel."

To the woman He said: "I will greatly multiply your sorrow and your conception; In pain you shall bring forth children; Your desire shall be for your husband, and he shall rule over you."

Then to Adam He said, "Because you have heeded the voice of your wife and have eaten from the tree of which I commanded you, saying, 'You shall not eat of it': Cursed is the ground for your sake; In toil you shall eat of it All the days of your life. Both thorns and

> *thistles it shall bring forth for you, and you shall eat the herb of the field. In the sweat of your face, you shall eat bread till you return to the ground, For out of it you were taken; For dust you are, And to dust you shall return."*
>
> *And Adam called his wife's name Eve because she was the mother of all living.*
>
> *Also, for Adam and his wife the LORD God made tunics of skin and clothed them.*
>
> *Then the LORD God said, "Behold, the man has become like one of Us, to know good and evil. And now, lest he put out his hand and take also of the tree of life, and eat, and live forever"—therefore the LORD God sent him out of the garden of Eden to till the ground from which he was taken. So, he drove out the man; and He placed cherubim at the east of the garden of Eden, and a flaming sword which turned every way, to guard the way to the tree of life. (Genesis 3 NKJV)*

In verses 11–24, God is conducting a trial of sort. He addresses each of the three—Adam, his wife, and the serpent. They are all found guilty and sentenced. I find it interesting that the serpent was included in the trial. Adam and Eve are cast out of the garden and must live and endure their punishment until they die and return to the ground. Mankind now has a sin problem that will be passed down through the generations. But God loves His people and continues to maintain His relationship with them. Ten generations later, in Genesis 6:5–7, God sees that man has become so wicked that He is grieved in His heart and says, *"I will destroy man whom I have created from the face of the earth."* But God finds one righteous man.

> *But Noah found grace in the eyes of the Lord. (Genesis 6:8 NKJV)*

God brings a great flood that destroys all the people and the creatures on the earth. But God saves Noah, his wife, their three sons, their wives, and a male and a female of each kind of creature on an ark to repopulate the earth. By the way, the great educator and author Dr. Henry Morris has calculated that there were over a billion people on the earth at the time of the flood (2348 BC). And again it looks like God had made a mistake giving man free will. I remind you that God is omniscient. He knew this was going to happen; He makes no mistakes. God knows that man has an inherent sinful nature, but He has a plan.

In Genesis 3:21, God made clothes for Adam and Eve to cover their nakedness. He could have made their clothes from plants or trees or wool, but He used the skin of an animal. This is very important. I believe that God killed an animal, probably a lamb, to cover them. Remember that Adam and Eve didn't realize they were naked until they sinned against God. God required the blood of a lamb to cover the sin of man. Therefore, the way God deals with our sin is through the blood of an innocent lamb. God provided the lamb in Genesis 3, and God will provide the Lamb to cover the sins of all mankind.

In Leviticus 9, during the forty years of "wilderness wandering," God speaks to Moses the prophet and told him to build an altar so the children of Israel could make atonement for their sins by sprinkling the blood of an animal on the altar.

> *Then Moses said, "This is the thing which the LORD commanded you to do, and the glory of the LORD will appear to you." And Moses said to Aaron, "Go to the altar, offer your sin offering and your burnt offering, and make atonement for yourself and for the people. Offer the offering of the people, and make atonement for them, as the LORD commanded." Aaron therefore went to the altar and killed the calf of the sin offering, which was for himself. Then the sons of Aaron brought the blood to him. And*

> *he dipped his finger in the blood, put it on the horns of the altar, and poured the blood at the base of the altar. (Leviticus 9:6–9 NKJV)*

These blood sacrifices would continue for years through the Old Testament. The sacrifice of the innocent lamb in Genesis 3 and the blood sacrifices after the Exodus were merely foreshadowing for something greater yet to come. For God, in His perfect plan and timing, was going to bring forth a Messiah who would save His people from their sin. The Old Testament books of Psalms, Isaiah, Jeremiah, Ezekiel, and Daniel are filled with prophecies of the coming Messiah.

> *Therefore, the Lord Himself will give you a sign: Behold, the virgin shall conceive and bear a Son, and shall call His name Immanuel. (Isaiah 7:14 NKJV)*

> *Know therefore and understand, that from the going forth of the command to restore and build Jerusalem Until Messiah the Prince, there shall be seven weeks and sixty-two weeks; The street shall be built again, and the wall, even in troublesome times. And after the sixty-two weeks Messiah shall be cut off, but not for Himself; And the people of the prince who is to come Shall destroy the city and the sanctuary. The end of it shall be with a flood, and till the end of the war desolations are determined. (Daniel 9:25–26 NKJV)*

> *But He was wounded for our transgressions, He was bruised for our iniquities; The chastisement for our peace was upon Him, And by His stripes we are healed. All we like sheep have gone astray; We have turned, everyone,*

to his own way; And the Lord has laid on Him the iniquity of us all. He was oppressed and He was afflicted, Yet He opened not His mouth; He was led as a lamb to the slaughter, and as a sheep before its shearers is silent, So He opened not His mouth. He was taken from prison and from judgment, and who will declare His generation? For He was cut off from the land of the living; For the transgressions of My people, He was stricken. And they made His grave with the wicked—But with the rich at His death, Because He had done no violence, nor was any deceit in His mouth. (Isaiah 53:5–9 NKJV)

THE STORY OF JESUS

The Life, Crucifixion, Resurrection, and Ascension of Jesus Christ

There was a four-hundred-year space between the Old and New Testaments of the Bible, when God stayed silent. When the New Testament begins, the Messiah, or Christ, will soon be born in Bethlehem Ephrathah, near Jerusalem.

> *But thou, Bethlehem Ephrathah, though thou be little among the thousands of Judah, yet out of thee shall he come forth unto me that is to be ruler in Israel; whose goings forth have been from of old, from everlasting. (Micah 5:2 KJV)*

The Christ is born of a virgin named Mary. It is believed that the sin nature was passed to the child through the father. Thus, Christ could have no earthly father. The virgin Mary was impregnated by the Holy Spirit; this is the Immaculate Conception.

> *Therefore, the Lord Himself will give you a sign: Behold, the virgin shall conceive and bear a Son, and shall call His name Immanuel. (Isaiah 7:14 KJV)*

Christ lived a sinless life.

> *And ye know that he was manifested to take away our sins; and in him is no sin. (1 John 3:5 KJV)*

Christ was fully God and fully man.

> *And the Word was made flesh, and dwelt among us, (and we beheld his glory, the glory as of the only begotten of the Father,) full of grace and truth. (John 1:14 KJV)*

God gave His Son, the Christ, the only sinless man to ever live, as an innocent, infinite sacrifice to cover every sin of the world. This is the Gospel.

> ***For God so loved the world, that he gave his only begotten Son, that whosoever believeth in him should not perish, but have everlasting life. (John 3:16 NKJV)***

After Christ Jesus died on the Roman cross, His body was placed in a tomb. He was resurrected on the third day.

> *But the angel answered and said to the women, "Do not be afraid, for I know that you seek Jesus who was crucified. He is not here; for He is risen, as He said. Come, see the place where the Lord lay." (Matthew 28:5–6 NKJV)*

Forty days after His resurrection, Christ ascends to heaven to be with His Father.

> *So then, after the Lord had spoken to them, He was received up into heaven, and sat*

down at the right hand of God. (Mark 16:19 NKJV)

Who has gone into heaven and is at the right hand of God, angels and authorities and powers having been made subject to Him. (1 Peter 3:22 NKJV)

The birth of Christ

Now in the sixth month the angel Gabriel was sent by God to a city of Galilee named Nazareth, to a virgin betrothed to a man whose name was Joseph, of the house of David. The virgin's name was Mary. And having come in, the angel said to her, "Rejoice, highly favored one, the Lord is with you; blessed are you among women!" But when she saw him, she was troubled at his saying, and considered what manner of greeting this was. Then the angel said to her, "Do not be afraid, Mary, for you have found favor with God. And behold, you will conceive in your womb and bring forth a Son and shall call His name JESUS. He will be great and will be called the Son of the Highest; and the Lord God will give Him the throne of His father David. And He will reign over the house of Jacob forever, and of His kingdom there will be no end." Then Mary said to the angel, "How can this be, since I do not know a man?" And the angel answered and said to her, "The Holy Spirit will come upon you, and the power of the Highest will overshadow you; therefore, also, that Holy One who is to be born will be called the Son of God." (Luke 1:26–35 NKJV)

And it came to pass in those days that a decree went out from Caesar Augustus that all the world should be registered. This census first took place while Quirinius was governing Syria. So, all went to be registered, everyone to his own city. Joseph also went up from Galilee, out of the city of Nazareth, into Judea, to the city of David, which is called Bethlehem, because he was of the house and lineage of David, to be registered with Mary, his betrothed wife, who was with child. So it was, that while they were there, the days were completed for her to be delivered. And she brought forth her firstborn Son, and wrapped Him in swaddling cloths, and laid Him in a manger, because there was no room for them in the inn.

Glory in the Highest

Now there were in the same country shepherds living out in the fields, keeping watch over their flock by night. And behold, an angel of the Lord stood before them, and the glory of the Lord shone around them, and they were greatly afraid. Then the angel said to them, "Do not be afraid, for behold, I bring you good tidings of great joy which will be to all people. For there is born to you this day in the city of David a Savior, who is Christ the Lord. And this will be the sign to you: You will find a Babe wrapped in swaddling cloths, lying in a manger." And suddenly there was with the angel a multitude of the heavenly host praising God and saying: "Glory to God in the highest, And on earth peace, goodwill toward men!" So it was, when the angels had gone away from them into heaven, that the shepherds said to one another, "Let us now go to Bethlehem and see this thing that has come to pass, which the Lord has made known to us." And they came with haste and found Mary and Joseph, and the Babe lying in a manger. Now when they had seen Him, they made widely known the saying which was told them concerning this Child. And all those who heard it marveled at those things which were told them by the shepherds. But Mary kept all these things and pondered them in her heart. Then the shepherds returned, glorifying and praising God for all the things that they had heard and seen, as it was told them.

Circumcision of Jesus

And when eight days were completed for the circumcision of the Child, His name was called JESUS, the name given by the angel before He was conceived in the womb.

Jesus Presented in the Temple

Now when the days of her purification according to the law of Moses were completed, they brought Him to Jerusalem to present Him to the Lord (as it is written in the law of the Lord, "Every male who opens the womb shall be called holy to the LORD"), and to offer a sacrifice according to what is said in the law of the Lord, "A pair of turtledoves or two young pigeons."

Simeon Sees God's Salvation

And behold, there was a man in Jerusalem whose name was Simeon, and this man was just and devout, waiting for the Consolation of Israel, and the Holy Spirit was upon him. And it had been revealed to him by the Holy Spirit that he would not see death before he had seen the Lord's Christ. So he came by the Spirit into the temple. And when the parents brought in the Child Jesus, to do for Him according to the custom of the law, he took Him up in his arms and blessed God and said: "Lord, now You are letting Your servant depart in peace, According to Your word; For my eyes have seen Your salvation Which You have prepared before the face of all peoples, A light to bring revelation to the Gentiles, And the glory of Your people Israel." And Joseph and His mother marveled at those things which were spoken of Him. Then Simeon blessed them, and said to Mary His mother, "Behold, this Child is destined for the fall and rising of many in Israel, and for a sign which will be spoken against (yes, a sword will pierce through your own soul also), that the thoughts of many hearts may be revealed."

Anna Bears Witness to the Redeemer

Now there was one, Anna, a prophetess, the daughter of Phanuel, of the tribe of Asher. She was of a great age and had lived with a husband seven years from her virginity; and this woman was a widow of about eighty-four years, who did not depart from the temple, but served God with fasting and prayers night

> *and day. And coming in that instant she gave thanks to the Lord and spoke of Him to all those who looked for redemption in Jerusalem.*
>
> *So, when they had performed all things according to the law of the Lord, they returned to Galilee, to their own city, Nazareth. And the Child grew and became strong in spirit, filled with wisdom; and the grace of God was upon Him. (Luke 2:1–40 NKJV)*

Jesus and His parents return to Nazareth, where He would grow up. The next time we read about Jesus, He is twelve years old. He and His parents are in Jerusalem for the Passover feast.

> *His parents went to Jerusalem every year at the Feast of the Passover. And when He was twelve years old, they went up to Jerusalem according to the custom of the feast. When they had finished the days, as they returned, the Boy Jesus lingered behind in Jerusalem. And Joseph and His mother did not know it; but supposing Him to have been in the company, they went a day's journey, and sought Him among their relatives and acquaintances. So, when they did not find Him, they returned to Jerusalem, seeking Him. Now so it was that after three days they found Him in the temple, sitting in the midst of the teachers, both listening to them and asking them questions. And all who heard Him were astonished at His understanding and answers. So when they saw Him, they were amazed; and His mother said to Him, "Son, why have You done this to us? Look, your father and I have sought You anxiously." And He said to them, **"Why did you seek Me? Did you not know that I must be***

> ***about My Father's business?"*** *But they did not understand the statement which He spoke to them." (Luke 2:41–50)*

Jesus and His parents again return home to Nazareth, where He was subject to them. He grew strong and wise there until about age thirty, when He begins His ministry.

Jesus begins His ministry

Jesus leaves Nazareth and goes to the river Jordan. He meets John the Baptizer there and is baptized. After His baptism, the Holy Spirit descends on Him, and the Father speaks from a cloud. The Holy Trinity is together on earth.

> *When all the people were baptized, it came to pass that Jesus also was baptized; and while He prayed, the heaven was opened. And the Holy Spirit descended in bodily form like a dove upon Him, and a voice came from heaven which said, "You are My beloved Son; in You I am well pleased." (Luke 3:21–22 NKJV)*

Afterward Jesus is led by the Spirit into the wilderness, where He fasts for forty days, then is tempted by the devil. After surviving the fast and defeating the devil, Jesus returns to Bethabara, where He had been baptized and is introduced by John the Baptizer as the Lamb of God (John 1:28–29). Here Jesus finds John, Andrew, and Peter; and they follow Him. They go to Bethsaida, where Jesus finds Philip and Nathanael, and they follow Him (John 1:43–51).

They then all go to Cana to a wedding, where Jesus preforms His first miracle. He turns water to wine (John 2:1–11). They then go down to Jerusalem for Passover; Jesus cleanses the temple by driving out the merchants and money changers with a whip (John 2:13–3:21). Also, Nicodemus, a Pharisee, comes by night to speak with Jesus.

They leave Jerusalem and go back to the Jordan, where Jesus's disciples are baptizing people (John 3:22–36), then to Samaria, where Jesus preaches to the woman at the well (John 4:1–42). They then go to Cana, where Jesus heals a nobleman's son in Capernaum, twenty-five miles away (John 4:42–54).

Then Jesus returns to Nazareth to teach in the synagogue there. Jesus taught well, but the people there knew Jesus as a child and would not accept Him as sent from God. The people rose in anger and were going to throw Jesus off a cliff, but He slipped away. These events are recorded in Luke chapters 3 and 4, where I notice something very important happens.

From the time Jesus meets John the Baptizer through when He returns to Nazareth, these events took place: Jesus was baptized in the Jordan. The Holy Spirit descended on Him. His Father praised Him from above. He was led into the wilderness, where He fasted forty days and was tempted by the devil. Jesus is introduced as the Lamb of God, cleanses the temple in Jerusalem, teaches Nicodemus and the woman at the well, and has a following of disciples. Due to these events, I believe that Jesus returned to Nazareth a very different man than before. He began teaching in the synagogue with authority. The people noticed this change and were confused and offended.

> *So, all those in the synagogue, when they heard these things, were filled with wrath, and rose up and thrust Him out of the city; and they led Him to the brow of the hill on which their city was built, that they might throw Him down over the cliff. Then passing through the midst of them, He went His way. (Luke 4:28–30)*

Jesus heads toward Capernaum, preaching the kingdom of God, teaching in the synagogues, healing the afflicted, and performing miracles. Jesus calls Peter, Andrew, James, and John into full-time discipleship and heals Peter's mother-in-law (Luke 4:31–42). Jesus and His disciples go into Capernaum, where He sees a tax collector named Matthew Levi. Jesus says to him, "Follow Me". Matthew left his work and followed Him. Jesus continued going about preaching and healing all who came to Him asking for help. He performed many miracles and fed the thousands who would gather to see and hear Him preach the kingdom of God, adding disciples as he went.

All the while, the holy men, the Pharisees, and the scribes were closely watching Jesus. They listened to what He taught and were confused and offended by His teachings and miracles because they were not exactly what they thought to be correct according to the law of Moses. The Pharisees and scribes knew from the Old Testament that the Messiah would come to save Israel, but they believed Jesus to be a radical and an impostor.

At the time, the nation of Israel was living under the authority of the Roman Empire. The Jewish people were heavily taxed by the Romans and had strict rules to live by in their own land. There was much animosity between the Jews and Romans, who were very harsh and cruel. Violators of Roman law were severely punished or crucified. The Jews were eagerly awaiting the promised Messiah, whom they thought would free them of the Roman oppression.

Jesus continued preaching and teaching and healing the afflicted throughout Israel. The high priest was told that Jesus had been healing on the Sabbath and claimed to be God. The priests met in secret and conspired to have Jesus killed. Jesus knew this was coming to pass and told His disciples that He would be going back to His Father soon but would return. They did not understand (Matthew 24).

> *Now as He sat on the Mount of Olives, the disciples came to Him privately, saying, "Tell us, when will these things be? And what will be the sign of Your coming, and of the end of the age?"*
>
> *And Jesus answered and said to them:* ***"Take heed that no one deceives you. For many will come in My name, saying, 'I am the Christ,' and will deceive many. And you***

will hear of wars and rumors of wars. See that you are not troubled; for all these things must come to pass, but the end is not yet. For nation will rise against nation, and kingdom against kingdom. And there will be famines, pestilences, and earthquakes in various places. All these are the beginning of sorrows.

"Then they will deliver you up to tribulation and kill you, and you will be hated by all nations for My name's sake. And then many will be offended, will betray one another, and will hate one another. Then many false prophets will rise up and deceive many. And because lawlessness will abound, the love of many will grow cold. But he who endures to the end shall be saved. And this gospel of the kingdom will be preached in all the world as a witness to all the nations, and then the end will come.

"Therefore, when you see the 'abomination of desolation,' spoken of by Daniel the prophet, standing in the holy place" (whoever reads, let him understand), "then let those who are in Judea flee to the mountains. Let him who is on the housetop not go down to take anything out of his house. And let him who is in the field not go back to get his clothes. But woe to those who are pregnant and to those who are nursing babies in those days! And pray that your flight may not be in winter or on the Sabbath. For then there will be great tribulation, such as has not been since the beginning of the world until this time, no, nor ever shall be. And unless those days were shortened, no flesh would be saved; but for the elect's sake those days will be shortened.

"Then if anyone says to you, 'Look, here is the Christ!' or 'There!' do not believe it. For false Christ's and false prophets will rise and show great signs and wonders to deceive, if possible, even the elect. See, I have told you beforehand.

"Therefore if they say to you, 'Look, He is in the desert!' do not go out; or 'Look, He is in the inner rooms!' do not believe it. For as the lightning comes from the east and flashes to the west, so also will the coming of the Son of Man be. For wherever the carcass is, there the eagles will be gathered together.

"Immediately after the tribulation of those days the sun will be darkened, and the moon will not give its light; the stars will fall from heaven, and the powers of the heavens will be shaken. Then the sign of the Son of Man will appear in heaven, and then all the tribes of the earth will mourn, and they will see the Son of Man coming on the clouds of heaven with power and great glory. And He will send His angels with a great sound of a trumpet, and they will gather together His elect from the four winds, from one end of heaven to the other.

"Now learn this parable from the fig tree: When its branch has already become tender and puts forth leaves, you know that summer is near. So, you also when you see all these things, know that it is near—at the doors! Assuredly, I say to you, this generation will by no means pass away till all these things take place. Heaven and earth will pass away, but My words will by no means pass away.

"But of that day and hour no one knows, not even the angels of heaven, but My Father only. But as the days of Noah were, so also will the coming of the Son of Man be. For as in the days before the flood, they were eating and drinking, marrying and giving in marriage, until the day that Noah entered the ark, and did not know until the flood came and took them all away, so also will the coming of the Son of Man be. Then two men will be in the field: one will be taken and the other left. Two women will be grinding at the mill: one will be taken and the other left. Watch therefore, for you do not know what hour your Lord is coming. But know this, that if the master of the house had known what hour the thief would come, he would have watched and not allowed his house to be broken into. Therefore, you also be ready, for the Son of Man is coming at an hour you do not expect." (Matthew 24:3–44 NKJV)

Now the Feast of Unleavened Bread drew near, which is called Passover. And the chief priests and the scribes sought how they might kill Him, for they feared the people. Then Satan entered Judas, surnamed Iscariot, who was numbered among the twelve. So he went his way and conferred with the chief priests and captains, how he might betray Him to them. And they were glad and agreed to give him money. So, he promised and sought opportunity to betray Him to them in the absence of the multitude. (Luke 22:1–6 NKJV)

According to Hebrew law, the day ends and the new day begins at sundown. Jesus sent Peter and John to go and prepare the Passover meal before sundown on Chamishi (Thursday), that they would eat after sundown, Shishi (Friday), Preparation Day.

> *Then came the Day of Unleavened Bread when the Passover must be killed. And He sent Peter and John, saying, **"Go and prepare the Passover for us, that we may eat."***
>
> *So, they said to Him, "Where do You want us to prepare?"*
>
> *And He said to them, **"Behold, when you have entered the city, a man will meet you carrying a pitcher of water; follow him into the house which he enters. Then you shall say to the master of the house, 'The Teacher says to you, "Where is the guest room where I may eat the Passover with My disciples?"' Then he will show you a large, furnished upper room; there make ready."***
>
> *So, they went and found it just as He had said, and they prepared the Passover. When the hour had come, He sat down, and the twelve apostles with Him.*
>
> *Then He said to them, **"With fervent desire I have desired to eat this Passover with you before I suffer; for I say to you, I will no longer eat of it until it is fulfilled in the kingdom of God."***
>
> ***Then He took the cup, and gave thanks, and said, "Take this and divide it among yourselves; for I say to you, I will not drink of the fruit of the vine until the kingdom of God comes."***
>
> *And He took bread, gave thanks, and broke it, and gave it to them, saying, **"This***

> *is* ***My body which is given for you; do this in remembrance of Me."***
>
> *Likewise He also took the cup after supper, saying,* ***"This cup is the new covenant in My blood, which is shed for you. But behold, the hand of My betrayer is with Me on the table. And truly the Son of Man goes as it has been determined, but woe to that man by whom He is betrayed!"***
>
> *Then they began to question among themselves, which of them it was who would do this thing. (Luke 22:7–23 NKJV)*

After this, Jesus and His disciples but one, Judas Iscariot, went out to the garden of Gethsemane to pray.

> *When He came to the place, He said to them,* ***"Pray that you may not enter into temptation."***
>
> *And He was withdrawn from them about a stone's throw, and He knelt down and prayed, saying,* ***"Father, if it is Your will, take this cup away from Me; nevertheless not My will, but Yours, be done."*** *Then an angel appeared to Him from heaven, strengthening Him. And being in agony, He prayed more earnestly. Then His sweat became like great drops of blood falling down to the ground.*
>
> *When He rose up from prayer, and had come to His disciples, He found them sleeping from sorrow. Then He said to them,* ***"Why do you sleep? Rise and pray, lest you enter into temptation."***
>
> *And while He was still speaking, behold, a multitude; and he who was called Judas, one of the twelve, went before them and drew near*

to Jesus to kiss Him. But Jesus said to him, ***"Judas, are you betraying the Son of Man with a kiss?"***

When those around Him saw what was going to happen, they said to Him, "Lord, shall we strike with the sword?" And one of them struck the servant of the high priest and cut off his right ear.

But Jesus answered and said, ***"Permit even this."*** *And He touched his ear and healed him.*

Then Jesus said to the chief priests, captains of the temple, and the elders who had come to Him, ***"Have you come out, as against a robber, with swords and clubs? When I was with you daily in the temple, you did not try to seize Me. But this is your hour, and the power of darkness."***

Having arrested Him, they led Him and brought Him into the high priest's house. But Peter followed at a distance. (Luke 22:40–54 NKJV)

Now the men who held Jesus mocked Him and beat Him. And having blindfolded Him, they struck Him on the face and asked Him, saying, "Prophesy! Who is the one who struck You?" And many other things they blasphemously spoke against Him.

As soon as it was day, the elders of the people, both chief priests and scribes, came together and led Him into their council, saying, "If You are the Christ, tell us."

But He said to them, ***"If I tell you, you will by no means believe. And if I also ask you, you will by no means answer Me or let Me go.***

> ***Hereafter the Son of Man will sit on the right hand of the power of God."***
>
> *Then they all said, "Are You then the Son of God?"*
>
> *So, He said to them,* ***"You rightly say that I am."***
>
> *And they said, "What further testimony do we need? For we have heard it ourselves from His own mouth." (Luke 22:63–71 NKJV)*

The Jews hand Jesus over to Pontius Pilate, the Roman prefect (governor) of Judaea, asking him to crucify Jesus.

> *Then the whole multitude of them arose and led Him to Pilate. And they began to accuse Him, saying, "We found this fellow perverting the nation, and forbidding to pay taxes to Caesar, saying that He Himself is Christ, a King."*
>
> *Then Pilate asked Him, saying, "Are You the King of the Jews?"*
>
> *He answered him and said,* ***"It is as you say."***
>
> *So, Pilate said to the chief priests and the crowd, "I find no fault in this Man."*
>
> *But they were the fiercer, saying, "He stirs up the people, teaching throughout all Judea, beginning from Galilee to this place."*
>
> *When Pilate heard of Galilee, he asked if the Man were a Galilean. And as soon as he knew that He belonged to Herod's jurisdiction, he sent Him to Herod, who was also in Jerusalem at that time. Now when Herod saw Jesus, he was exceedingly glad; for he had desired for a long time to see Him, because he had heard many things about Him, and he*

> *hoped to see some miracle done by Him. Then he questioned Him with many words, but He answered him nothing. And the chief priests and scribes stood and vehemently accused Him. Then Herod, with his men of war, treated Him with contempt and mocked Him, arrayed Him in a gorgeous robe, and sent Him back to Pilate. (Luke 23:1–11 NKJV)*

Pilate finds no fault in Jesus

> *Then Pilate, when he had called together the chief priests, the rulers, and the people, said to them, "You have brought this Man to me, as one who misleads the people. And indeed, having examined Him in your presence, I have found no fault in this Man concerning those things of which you accuse Him; no, neither did Herod, for I sent you back to him; and indeed nothing deserving of death has been done by Him. I will therefore chastise Him and release Him" (for it was necessary for him to release one to them at the feast).*
>
> *And they all cried out at once, saying, "Away with this Man, and release to us Barabbas"—who had been thrown into prison for a certain rebellion made in the city, and for murder.*
>
> *Pilate, therefore, wishing to release Jesus, again called out to them. But they shouted, saying, "Crucify Him, crucify Him!"*
>
> *Then he said to them the third time, "Why, what evil has He done? I have found no reason for death in Him. I will therefore chastise Him and let Him go."*

> *But they were insistent, demanding with loud voices that He be crucified. And the voices of these men and of the chief priests prevailed. So Pilate gave sentence that it should be as they requested. And he released to them the one they requested, who for rebellion and murder had been thrown into prison; but he delivered Jesus to their will. (Luke 23:13–25 NKJV)*

Jesus is crucified

> *Now as they led Him away, they laid hold of a certain man, Simon a Cyrenian, who was coming from the country, and on him they laid the cross that he might bear it after Jesus.*
>
> *And a great multitude of the people followed Him, and women who also mourned and lamented Him. But Jesus, turning to them, said,* ***"Daughters of Jerusalem, do not weep for Me, but weep for yourselves and for your children. For indeed the days are coming in which they will say, 'Blessed are the barren, wombs that never bore, and breasts which never nursed!' Then they will begin 'to say to the mountains, "Fall on us!" and to the hills, "Cover us!"' For if they do these things in the green wood, what will be done in the dry?"***
>
> *There were also two others, criminals, led with Him to be put to death. And when they had come to the place called Calvary, there they crucified Him, and the criminals, one on the right hand and the other on the left. Then Jesus said,* ***"Father, forgive them, for they do not know what they do."***

And they divided His garments and cast lots. And the people stood looking on. But even the rulers with them sneered, saying, "He saved others; let Him save Himself if He is the Christ, the chosen of God."

The soldiers also mocked Him, coming and offering Him sour wine, and saying, "If You are the King of the Jews, save Yourself."

And an inscription also was written over Him in letters of Greek, Latin, and Hebrew:

THIS IS THE KING OF THE JEWS.

Then one of the criminals who were hanged blasphemed Him, saying, "If You are the Christ, save Yourself and us."

But the other, answering, rebuked him, saying, "Do you not even fear God, seeing you are under the same condemnation? And we indeed justly, for we receive the due reward of our deeds; but this Man has done nothing wrong." Then he said to Jesus, "Lord, remember me when You come into Your kingdom."

And Jesus said to him, ***"Assuredly, I say to you, today you will be with Me in Paradise."***

Now it was about the sixth hour, and there was darkness over all the earth until the ninth hour. Then the sun was darkened, and the veil of the temple was torn in two. And when Jesus had cried out with a loud voice, He said, ***"Father, 'into Your hands I commit My spirit.'"*** *Having said this, He breathed His last.*

So, when the centurion saw what had happened, he glorified God, saying, "Certainly this was a righteous Man!"

> *And the whole crowd who came together to that sight, seeing what had been done, beat their breasts and returned. But all His acquaintances, and the women who followed Him from Galilee, stood at a distance, watching these things. (Luke 23:26–49)*

Joseph of Arimathea and Nicodemus took down the body of Jesus and placed Him in Joseph's tomb.

> *After this, Joseph of Arimathea, being a disciple of Jesus, but secretly, for fear of the Jews, asked Pilate that he might take away the body of Jesus; and Pilate gave him permission. So, he came and took the body of Jesus. And Nicodemus, who at first came to Jesus by night, also came, bringing a mixture of myrrh and aloes, about a hundred pounds. Then they took the body of Jesus and bound it in strips of linen with the spices, as the custom of the Jews is to bury. Now in the place where He was crucified there was a garden, and in the garden a new tomb in which no one had yet been laid. So, there they laid Jesus, because of the Jews' Preparation Day, for the tomb was nearby. (John 19:38–42 NKJV)*

The body of Jesus was placed in the tomb, and a large stone was set in place to block the entrance before sundown on Preparation Day, Shishi (Friday). The following day was the Passover Sabbath day, Shabbat (Saturday), a day of rest according to Jewish law. The next day was Rishon (Sunday), the first day of the week and the day Jesus rose from the dead. Some believe that Jesus was crucified on Revi'i (Wednesday). This is possible with an additional Sabbath or High Sabbath on Chamishi (Thursday), Passover Day. This would allow for three days and three nights in the tomb as Jesus said He would be in Matthew 12:40.

The resurrection

> *Now after the Sabbath, as the first day of the week began to dawn, Mary Magdalene and the other Mary came to see the tomb. And behold, there was a great earthquake; for an angel of the Lord descended from heaven and came and rolled back the stone from the door, and sat on it. His countenance was like lightning, and his clothing as white as snow. And the guards shook for fear of him and became like dead men.*
>
> *But the angel answered and said to the women, "Do not be afraid, for I know that you seek Jesus who was crucified. He is not here; for He is risen, as He said. Come, see the place where the Lord lay. And go quickly and tell His disciples that He is risen from the dead, and indeed He is going before you into Galilee; there you will see Him. Behold, I have told you."*
>
> *So, they went out quickly from the tomb with fear and great joy and ran to bring His disciple's word.*
>
> *And as they went to tell His disciples, behold, Jesus met them, saying,* ***"Rejoice!"*** *So, they came and held Him by the feet and worshiped Him. Then Jesus said to them,* ***"Do not be afraid. Go and tell My brethren to go to Galilee, and there they will see Me." (Matthew 28:1–10 NKJV)***

The Great Commission

Then the eleven disciples went away into Galilee, to the mountain which Jesus had appointed for them. When they saw Him, they worshiped Him; but some doubted.

And Jesus came and spoke to them, saying, ***"All authority has been given to Me in heaven and on earth. Go therefore and make disciples of all the nations, baptizing them in the name of the Father and of the Son and of the Holy Spirit, teaching them to observe all things that I have commanded you; and lo, I am with you always, even to the end of the age."*** *Amen. (Matthew 28:16–20 NKJV)*

Jesus ascends unto heaven

The former account I made, O Theophilus, of all that Jesus began both to do and teach, until the day in which He was taken up, after He through the Holy Spirit had given commandments to the apostles whom He had chosen, to whom He also presented Himself alive after His suffering by many infallible proofs, being seen by them during forty days and speaking of the things pertaining to the kingdom of God.

And being assembled together with them, He commanded them not to depart from Jerusalem, but to wait for the Promise of the Father, "which," He said, ***"You have heard from Me; for John truly baptized with water, but you shall be baptized with the Holy Spirit not many days from now."*** *Therefore, when they had come together, they asked Him, say-*

ing, "Lord, will You at this time restore the kingdom to Israel?" And He said to them, ***"It is not for you to know times or seasons which the Father has put in His own authority.***

But you shall receive power when the Holy Spirit has come upon you; and you shall be witnesses to Me in Jerusalem, and in all Judea and Samaria, and to the end of the earth."

Now when He had spoken these things, while they watched, He was taken up, and a cloud received Him out of their sight. And while they looked steadfastly toward heaven as He went up, behold, two men stood by them in white apparel, who also said, "Men of Galilee, why do you stand gazing up into heaven? This same Jesus, who was taken up from you into heaven, will so come in like manner as you saw Him go into heaven." (Acts 1:1–11 NKJV)

SALVATION

First let me tell you this fact that everyone needs to understand and accept. Every person that has ever been, or will be conceived, will have eternal life. They will either be saved to be with God in the New Jerusalem (heaven) or condemned and cast into the lake of fire (hell). Let me make this more personal. You will spend eternity in either heaven or hell. There is no other option—one or the other forever.

I believe that God intends for everyone to be with Him in His kingdom forever after heaven and earth pass away. I also believe that the lake of fire in Revelation 20 is for the devil, the beast, and the false profit. However, many human souls will also be cast into the lake of fire. Let's examine these verses:

> *Then I saw a great white throne and Him who sat on it, from whose face the earth and the heaven fled away. And there was found no place for them. And I saw the dead, small and great, standing before God, and books were opened. And another book was opened, which is the Book of Life. And the dead were judged according to their works, by the things which were written in the books. The sea gave up the dead who were in it, and Death and Hades delivered up the dead who were in them. And they were judged, each one according to his works. Then Death and Hades were cast into the lake of fire. This is the second death. And anyone not found written in the Book of*

> *Life was cast into the lake of fire. (Revelation 20:11–15 NKJV)*

This is the white throne of judgment, where only those who have not been saved will stand and be judged. They will be "judged according to their works" because they will not receive the grace of God that He gives to those who accept Christ, for they never knew Him. It saddens me to write about this.

Verse 12 states, "And books were opened." These books are a record of everyone's life. Every action, every word spoken, and even every thought they have had is recorded in these books. These books will be filled with the daily accounts of the lost. Each soul there will stand in judgment as his or her entire life is reviewed.

Every person judged at the white throne will be guilty of at least one sin, probably many more than one, but it only takes one sin to make a person guilty of sin. And then the Book of Life will be opened to see if that person's name is written in that book. No one who will be judged at the white throne judgment will be found in the Book of Life. Verse 15 is very clear that all not found written in the Book of Life will be cast into the lake of fire. No one knows what this will be like; but Billy Graham, in a sermon, said that he thought it would be

> completely alone in total darkness forever, and an unquenchable fire would burn inside each soul longing to be in the presence of the loving God.

I agree with his theory.

God loves every person more than our human minds can comprehend. This is known as agape love.

> *But God demonstrates His own love toward us, in that while we were still sinners, Christ died for us. (Romans 5:8 NKJV)*

God has bent over backward for us; He gave His only Son so that no one should ever be cast into the lake of fire.

> ***For God so loved the world that He gave His only begotten Son, that whoever believes in Him should not perish but have everlasting life. For God did not send His Son into the world to condemn the world, but that the world through Him might be saved. (John 3:16–17 NKJV)***

The Almighty God is preparing to host a celebration greater than anyone can imagine that will never end, and He wants you there too. Let's talk about how you get your invitation.

How are we to be saved?

The definition of *saved* is "set aside, stored, or preserved for later use" and, in religion, "delivered from sin and from spiritual death: rescued from eternal punishment" (*Merriam-Webster Dictionary*).

The apostle Paul tells us, ***"For the wages of sin is death; but the gift of God is eternal life through Jesus Christ our Lord" (Romans 6:23 KJV)***.

To be saved is to be rescued from our sin that would lead us to eternal damnation.

Remember earlier I wrote that God would provide the Lamb that would cover the sins of all mankind? The Lamb of God is the Messiah—His Son, Jesus Christ. And that Jesus was born of a virgin and had no earthly father and therefore had no inherent sin nature. Jesus was fully man and fully God and never once sinned. Jesus is the perfect innocent, infinite sacrifice that, through His precious blood, covered the sin of all who believe in Him. Jesus is the only man that was born to die.

> ***For He made Him who knew no sin to be sin for us, that we might become the righ-***

> *teousness of God in Him. (2 Corinthians 5:21 NKJV)*
>
> *In this is love, not that we loved God, but that He loved us and sent His Son to be the propitiation for our sins. (1 John 4:10 NKJV)*

The Gospel in my words and understanding

God made man in His image and gave him dominion over all His creation. God's love for mankind is powerful, more powerful than we can comprehend. God gave man free will to choose to love and obey Him or to serve himself. Man chose to disobey God by doing the one thing God forbid him to do. Man ate of the tree of knowledge of good and evil.

This disobedience or sin altered the relationship between man and God forever. All mankind now is born with a sinful nature; but God, being holy, cannot be in the presence of unrighteousness or sin. So God sent His Son to live in the world in the flesh of a human man to teach us how to live, how to worship God, and how to repent from sin and be saved. Then God sent His Son, Jesus, the only man without blemish (sin), to die as the perfect sacrifice to cover the sins of all mankind.

While Jesus hung on the cross, God took all our sins and put them on Him. Jesus took all the pain that we deserve upon Himself so that we should not feel the sting of death. We all deserve the cross, but Jesus endured the cross in our place out of love for all mankind. Jesus hung on that cross for six hours before He took His last breath and died.

Most criminals who were crucified in those days died from asphyxiation because they became so fatigued they could no longer draw a breath of air, but modern science has proven that Jesus actually died of blood loss due to the extensive scourging that He endured before He was nailed to the cross.

His body was taken down and put into a sealed tomb before sundown the day before Passover Shabbat. On the third day, the Lord

Jesus Christ arose from the dead as He said He would and appeared to His disciples and the women that had followed and cared for Him. For forty days, Jesus met with and taught His disciples about things to come. He commissioned His disciples to go out and tell the whole world.

> ***He who believes and is baptized will be saved; but he who does not believe will be condemned. (Mark 16:16 NKJV)***

He then ascended into heaven to His Father. This is the Gospel of Jesus Christ.

These next words are the most important of this book and likely the most important words I will ever write. You have just read what God did for your salvation. The question now is, What must we do in response?

We must come to the cross of Jesus, where He alone paid the price of our sin. Jesus went to the cross for all. He did not have to endure the agonizing death; He did it all for us because He loves us. It is only at the cross of Jesus that we find forgiveness of sins. We must humble ourselves and submit to Him and make Jesus Lord of our lives. *Lord* means "owner" or "master."

We must become bond servants of Christ. We must willingly give our lives over to Him as lifetime servants—His will over our own. I have heard pastors say that salvation is easy. "Just believe and be saved." This statement is just wrong and a contradiction to the Scriptures. Jesus said in Matthew that it is difficult to follow Him.

> ***Enter by the narrow gate; for wide is the gate and broad is the way that leads to destruction, and there are many who go in by it. Because narrow is the gate and difficult is the way which leads to life, and there are few who find it. (Matthew 7:13–14 NKJV)***

In the Gospels of Matthew, Mark, and Luke, a rich young ruler asks Jesus what he must do to have eternal life. Jesus tells him that he must keep the Commandments and to give his riches to the poor and follow Him.

> *Now a certain ruler asked Him, saying, "Good Teacher, what shall I do to inherit eternal life?" So, Jesus said to him,* ***"Why do you call Me good? No one is good but one, that is, God. You know the commandments: 'Do not commit adultery,' 'Do not murder,' 'Do not steal,' 'Do not bear false witness,' 'Honor your father and your mother.'"*** *And he said, "All these things I have kept from my youth." So, when Jesus heard these things, He said to him,* ***"You still lack one thing. Sell all that you have and distribute to the poor, and you will have treasure in heaven; and come, follow Me."*** *But when he heard this, he became very sorrowful, for he was very rich. (Luke 18:18–23 NKJV)*

Let's examine more scriptures where Jesus is speaking on salvation.

> ***Most assuredly, I say to you, he who hears My word and believes in Him who sent Me has everlasting life, and shall not come into judgment, but has passed from death into life. (John 5:24 NKJV)***

> ***All that the Father gives Me will come to Me, and the one who comes to Me I will by no means cast out. (John 6:37 NKJV)***

> *Jesus said to her,* ***"I am the resurrection and the life. He who believes in Me, though he***

may die, he shall live. And whoever lives and believes in Me shall never die. Do you believe this?" (John 11:25–26 NKJV)

And I give them eternal life, and they shall never perish; neither shall anyone snatch them out of My hand. (John 10:28 NKJV)

Not everyone who says to Me, "Lord, Lord," shall enter the kingdom of heaven, but he who does the will of My Father in heaven. Many will say to Me in that day, "Lord, Lord, have we not prophesied in Your name, cast out demons in Your name, and done many wonders in Your name?" And then I will declare to them, "I never knew you; depart from Me, you who practice lawlessness!" (Matthew 7:21–23 NKJV)

Jesus said to him, "I am the way, the truth, and the life. No one comes to the Father except through Me." (John 14:6 NKJV)

No one can come to Me unless the Father who sent Me draws him; and I will raise him up at the last day. (John 6:44 NKJV)

Believing in Christ means that we trust in Him, that He is who He says He is and that He will do what He says He will do. Believing also requires a commitment to Him. Christ demands to be first in our lives and that we cannot serve two masters and that we must commit ourselves to Him. It is also a motivation for service—a motivation to go out into the world and help the poor and the hungry and preach the Gospel. We must be "born again" and become a new creation through Christ.

I like to go out and knock on doors to meet people to invite them to church and share the Gospel with them, if they will hear it. For those who will listen, I will explain what it means to be born again. I then open my Bible to the Gospel of John chapter 3, the conversation between Jesus and Nicodemus. Jesus is teaching Nicodemus that a man must be born again to see the kingdom of God.

> *There was a man of the Pharisees named Nicodemus, a ruler of the Jews. This man came to Jesus by night and said to Him, "Rabbi, we know that You are a teacher come from God; for no one can do these signs that You do unless God is with him."*
>
> *Jesus answered and said to him,* ***"Most assuredly, I say to you, unless one is born again, he cannot see the kingdom of God."***
>
> *Nicodemus said to Him, "How can a man be born when he is old? Can he enter a second time into his mother's womb and be born?"*
>
> *Jesus answered,* ***"Most assuredly, I say to you, unless one is born of water and the Spirit, he cannot enter the kingdom of God. That which is born of the flesh is flesh, and that which is born of the Spirit is spirit. Do not marvel that I said to you, 'You must be born again.' The wind blows where it wishes, and you hear the sound of it, but cannot tell where it comes from and where it goes. So is everyone who is born of the Spirit."***
>
> *Nicodemus answered and said to Him, "How can these things be?"*
>
> *Jesus answered and said to him,* ***"Are you the teacher of Israel, and do not know these things? Most assuredly, I say to you, we speak what We know and testify what We have seen, and you do not receive Our witness. If I have***

> *told you earthly things and you do not believe, how will you believe if I tell you heavenly things? No one has ascended to heaven but He who came down from heaven, that is, the Son of Man who is in heaven. And as Moses lifted up the serpent in the wilderness, even so must the Son of Man be lifted up, that whoever believes in Him should not perish but have eternal life. For God so loved the world that He gave His only begotten Son, that whoever believes in Him should not perish but have everlasting life. For God did not send His Son into the world to condemn the world, but that the world through Him might be saved.*
>
> *"He who believes in Him is not condemned; but he who does not believe is condemned already, because he has not believed in the name of the only begotten Son of God. And this is the condemnation, that the light has come into the world, and men loved darkness rather than light, because their deeds were evil. For everyone practicing evil hates the light and does not come to the light, lest his deeds should be exposed. But he who does the truth comes to the light, that his deeds may be clearly seen, that they have been done in God." (John 3:1–21 NKJV)*

I believe this secret meeting and dialogue of Jesus and Nicodemus is very important because this is Jesus's first visit to Jerusalem in His ministry. Jesus had just recently cleansed the temple and driven out the money changers with a whip. This caused quite a ruckus and had everyone talking. Nicodemus becomes curious about Jesus and requests this private meeting at night. At the time, Nicodemus is a Pharisee and a member of the Sanhedrin, only second to Caiaphas, the chief priest of Israel. Nicodemus was the equivalent of a theological professor of Jewish law and the Torah.

Jesus is telling Nicodemus that, when one comes to know Christ, he is to be born again; but he is not understanding because this is all new to him. We don't know if Nicodemus knew that Jesus was the Messiah at the time, but I believe he eventually came to realize it later. From this conversation, we learn that, to be saved, we must be born again spiritually—become a new creation in Christ.

The word *repent* means to turn and go the opposite direction. Jesus commands us to repent of our sins. We should stop what we are doing in our lives that is sinful and move toward righteousness and change our minds from fleshly desires to heavenly desires.

> *From that time Jesus began to preach and to say, "Repent, for the kingdom of heaven is at hand." (Matthew 4:17 NKJV)*

> *The Lord is not slack concerning His promise, as some count slackness, but is longsuffering toward us, not willing that any should perish but that all should come to repentance. (2 Peter 3:9 NKJV)*

One more term we need to define—*the elect*. This term has caused confusion for many. *The elect* is used twenty-four times in twenty-three verses in the New Testament. *The elect* means the same as *the chosen*, which is referring to the church or the followers of Christ.

> *For false Christs and false prophets will rise and show great signs and wonders to deceive, if possible, even the elect. (Matthew 24:24 NKJV)*

We now should understand what we must do to receive eternal life through Christ. We must know Him and have a personal relationship with our Lord. We must come to the cross, humble ourselves, and praise Him and thank Him for what He endured for us at the cross. We must believe in Him, put our trust in Him, and do His will. We must take up our own cross and follow Him.

When we arrive at the point where our relationship with God or Christ is our top priority, only then can we be sure that we are truly saved and will have eternal life in the kingdom of God.

What changes when we are saved?

The moment we ask Jesus to be our Lord and Savior and He knows we are sincere, the Holy Spirit will indwell us and live within our hearts.

> ***In Him you also trusted, after you heard the word of truth, the gospel of your salvation; in whom also, having believed, you were sealed with the Holy Spirit of promise, who is the guarantee of our inheritance until the redemption of the purchased possession, to the praise of His glory. (Ephesians 1:13–14 NKJV)***

Some religions teach that it is possible to lose our salvation. According to Scripture, one cannot lose salvation.

> ***And I give them eternal life, and they shall never perish; neither shall anyone snatch them out of My hand. (John 10:28 NKJV)***

At the time of salvation, you receive the seal of God on your head.

> ***Do not labor for the food which perishes, but for the food which endures to everlasting life, which the Son of Man will give you,***

because God the Father has set His seal on Him. (John 6:27 NKJV)

They were commanded not to harm the grass of the earth, or any green thing, or any tree, but only those men who do not have the seal of God on their foreheads. (Revelation 9:4 NKJV)

COME TO THE CROSS

Charity Gayle

Come follow Me, I heard Him say
Come follow Me, I'll show you the way
Leave all behind, I'll grant you treasure on high
Come follow Me, leave all behind
Come to the cross where sinners are saved
Come to the cross where all debts are paid
Here at the cross the Son of God gave His life
Here at the cross, come to the cross
Come and behold, see where He lay
Come and behold an empty grave
He is alive; there's victory in Jesus Christ
Come and behold, He is alive.
With the Spirit's power dwelling now within
We will take our cross, we will follow Him
And tell the world of His cleansing blood
And that through the cross we have overcome
With the Spirit's power dwelling now within
We will take our cross, we will follow Him
And tell the world of His cleansing blood
And that through the cross we have overcome
Come to the cross, come and be safe
Come to the cross where sin's washed away
Fall on your knees before the Lord God Most High
Fall on your knees, give up your life
Fall on your knees, give up your life

BELIEVER'S BAPTISM

Do we have to be baptized to be saved?

Believer's baptism is very important; the Bible commands it. Let's consider these scriptures. This is Jesus speaking:

> ***Go therefore and make disciples of all the nations, baptizing them in the name of the Father and of the Son and of the Holy Spirit. (Matthew 28:19 NKJV)***

> ***He who believes and is baptized will be saved; but he who does not believe will be condemned. (Mark 16:16 NKJV)***

In these two verses, Jesus clearly wants, or rather commands, believers to be baptized soon after they make a personal decision to follow Him. Jesus Himself was baptized and received the anointing of the Holy Spirit in public. Baptism is a public profession of faith that one is a follower of Christ. The believer is submerged in water in the name of the Father, and of the Son, and of the Holy Spirit. This work of faith symbolizes the death, burial, and resurrection of Jesus Christ. The act of baptism is **not** what saves the believer but is the first act of obedience after accepting Christ as Savior. Christ said, "***Believe and be baptized.***"

I believe that baptism should be done publicly, with the church as witnesses. Everyone Jesus called, He called publicly. Jesus said:

> ***Therefore whoever confesses Me before men, him I will also confess before My Father who is in heaven. (Matthew 10:32 NKJV)***

Witnessing a believer's baptism can also lead the lost to accepting Christ as well.

The church of Christ, however, teaches that the believer is saved at the time of baptism and that the Holy Spirit indwells and anoints the believer at that moment. This is not biblical. Baptism is an act or work of obedience by the believer. The Bible tells us that we are saved by grace, not by works.

> ***For it is by grace you have been saved, through faith—and this is not from yourselves, it is the gift of God—not by works, so that no one can boast. (Ephesians 2:8–9 NIV)***

The Baptist church, along with many nondenominational church doctrines, call for believers' water baptism only as an act of obedience or a good work of faith and strongly encouraged only after being saved by the grace of God.

The Catholic, Presbyterian, and Lutheran churches conduct infant baptisms. This is not biblical. The Bible scriptures are clear that first one must believe and then be baptized. These three churches also baptize adults but by sprinkling.

The Methodist church and others sprinkle water on the heads of the believers instead of submersion. This is not biblical. The word *baptize* is a translation of the Greek word *baptizo*, which is related to the verb *bapto*, which means "to dip" as in to dye cloth in color by dipping or submerging. Also, Jesus was submerged in the Jordan River at His baptism. I believe that we should be submerged in water to represent the death, burial, and resurrection of Christ.

I personally know many Christians that have never been baptized for whatever reason. By not being baptized, they are telling Christ, "Jesus, thanks for dying on the cross for my salvation, but I'm not willing to be baptized as You commanded." Being followers of Christ, we should honor Him by following Him in baptism, if one is physically able. If someone was not willing to carry out Jesus's first command, I would question if they were actually saved. The Bible tells us that faith without works is dead.

> *For as the body without the spirit is dead, so faith without works is dead also. (James 2:26 NKJV)*

To answer the original question, no, you don't have to be baptized to be saved. But my question to you is, Why wouldn't you be baptized?

My personal experience of baptism

Some of my earliest memories are of being in the First Methodist Church in my hometown. I'm so grateful that I was raised by Christian parents who had me in church as a young child. When I was nine or ten years old, my mother told me it was time for me to be baptized.

I remember, for the next few weeks, instead of being in Sunday school, I went to a small class with a few others in the pastor's office. We learned what it meant to be baptized and that I was going to "join the church." I thought that meant that I would be on the church role as a member of that church. I realized years later that I had misunderstood what the pastor meant by "joining the church." I learned that I was joining the church of Jesus Christ, as in the bride of Christ. A few Sundays later, our class was called to the front of the church to be baptized. We were each introduced to the church and sprinkled on the head with holy water, and we received our own Bible.

Years later, when I was twenty-six, I was attending a revival at a Baptist church when I realized that I had not been baptized properly.

I knew that I was saved but needed to be baptized in accordance with the Bible. You see, in the Methodist church, I was not submerged in water; nor did I fully understand exactly what it meant to be baptized. Parents should make sure that their children understand fully what baptism means before encouraging them to be baptized.

At the end of the revival, I was baptized properly. I was immersed in water in the name of the Father, and of the Son, and of the Holy Spirit before the church. It took me some time, but I did it the right way. God was glorified.

> *Buried with Him in baptism, in which you also were raised with Him through faith in the working of God, who raised Him from the dead. (Colossians 2:12 NKJV)*

> *And now why are you waiting? Arise and be baptized, and wash away your sins, calling on the name of the Lord. (Acts 22:16 NKJV)*

WHY GOD ALLOWS SATAN TO EXIST

The actual name of Satan, or the devil, is Lucifer (light bearer). God created Lucifer as His most high angel. He was beautiful, very intelligent, and powerful. He was, in essence, commander in chief of God's army of angels. Lucifer was very proud of his stature and power but became envious and jealous of God's honor and glory. The scriptures Ezekiel 28:11–19 and Isaiah 14:12–17 tell us more about Lucifer.

I want to remind you that God is omniscient; He had full knowledge of this beforehand. Lucifer began to rebel and attempted to overthrow God. Angels also have free will. The Almighty God cast Lucifer down to the ground (earth, not hell) and took away his position in heaven but not his powers and intelligence. He was free to move about on earth and heaven. It makes you wonder why God didn't just destroy him, right? God allows Lucifer to exist for a time, coincidentally almost the same amount of time as man will live on the earth.

We know that this all took place sometime before Adam and the woman lived in the garden in Genesis 3. After Lucifer was banished from his position in heaven, he was, and is, very angry. He wants revenge against God but knows he is powerless against the Almighty. So he has set his sights on the next best target—God's beloved people. Satan knows the Bible, and he knows what awaits him in Revelation 20. And he wants to take you and me with him to the lake of fire. Until then, he wants to destroy lives, families, and churches. He is very intelligent and clever and has no remorse. He uses lust of the flesh, drugs, and alcohol to destroy our children and our marriages. His goal is to get God's people to worship him, and he knows the best ways and times to tempt us. So

> *be sober, be vigilant; because your adversary the devil, as a roaring lion, walketh about, seeking whom he may devour:*
>
> *Who resist steadfast in the faith, knowing that the same afflictions are accomplished in your brethren that are in the world. (1 Peter 5:8–9 KJV)*

Back to Genesis 3, Satan enters the serpent to tempt Adam's wife. Satan is talking with her and cleverly causing her to question God's command not to eat of "the tree in the midst of the garden" and persuades her to eat. She then gave the fruit to Adam, and he also ate. The question we must ask ourselves is, Would she have disobeyed God had Satan not been there to tempt her? I say, no, she would not have eaten of the tree. I believe that, if Satan had never entered the garden, Adam and Eve would still be there living today.

I believe that God allows Satan to exist because He gave man free will to choose between righteousness or evil. Without temptation, there would be no choice to make. I believe that God wants us to make a conscious decision and choose to serve Him over sin. Satan brought sin into the world, and God allowed it. God is holy and righteous; Satan is evil and deceptive. Satan's presence in the world gives us a contrast to God and forces man to make a choice. Each day, we all must make a choice: "Will I live for God, or will I live for Satan?"

Satan knows his time is short; and he is coming to steal, kill, and destroy lives. Prepare yourselves for his unrelenting attacks. Never engage in a conversation with the devil, and instead, pray for God to protect you. Satan will flee from you, but he will return again sometime.

> *Put on the whole armor of God, that you may be able to stand against the schemes of the devil. (Ephesians 6:11 ESV)*

Moreover, the word of the Lord came to me, saying, "Son of man, take up a lamentation for the king of Tyre, and say to him, 'Thus says the Lord God:

"You were the seal of perfection, Full of wisdom and perfect in beauty. You were in Eden, the garden of God; Every precious stone was your covering: The sardius, topaz, and diamond, Beryl, onyx, and jasper, Sapphire, turquoise, and emerald with gold. The workmanship of your timbrels and pipes Was prepared for you on the day you were created.

"You were the anointed cherub who covers; I established you; You were on the holy mountain of God; You walked back and forth in the midst of fiery stones. You were perfect in your ways from the day you were created, till iniquity was found in you.

"By the abundance of your trading You became filled with violence within, and you sinned; Therefore, I cast you as a profane thing Out of the mountain of God; And I destroyed you, O covering cherub, From the midst of the fiery stones.

"Your heart was lifted up because of your beauty; You corrupted your wisdom for the sake of your splendor; I cast you to the ground, I laid you before kings, that they might gaze at you.

"You defiled your sanctuaries by the multitude of your iniquities, By the iniquity of your trading; Therefore, I brought fire from your midst; It devoured you, And I turned you to ashes upon the earth in the sight of all who saw you. All who knew you among the peoples are astonished at you; You have become a hor-

ror and shall be no more forever.'"'" (Ezekiel 28:11–19 NKJV)

How you are fallen from heaven, O Lucifer, son of the morning! How you are cut down to the ground, you who weakened the nations! For you have said in your heart: "I will ascend into heaven, I will exalt my throne above the stars of God; I will also sit on the mount of the congregation on the farthest sides of the north; I will ascend above the heights of the clouds, I will be like the Most High." Yet you shall be brought down to Sheol, To the lowest depths of the Pit.

Those who see you will gaze at you, and consider you, saying: "Is this the man who made the earth tremble, who shook kingdoms, who made the world as a wilderness and destroyed its cities, who did not open the house of his prisoners?" (Isaiah 14:12–17 NKJV)

The devil, who deceived them, was cast into the lake of fire and brimstone where the beast and the false prophet are. And they will be tormented day and night forever and ever. (Revelation 20:10 NKJV)

THE BOOK OF JOB

Have you read the book of Job? Did you know that the book of Job is probably the oldest book ever written? Did you know that Job is considered by many influential authors, philosophers, and theologians to be a masterpiece? This is true.

> One of the grandest things ever written with pen. There is nothing written, I think, of equal literary merit. (Thomas Carlyle)

> The book of Job is perhaps the greatest masterpiece of the human mind. (Victor Hugo)

> More magnificent and sublime than any other book of scripture. (Martin Luther)

> The greatest poem, whether of ancient or modern literature. (Alfred Lord Tennyson)

> A magnificent dramatic poem acknowledged as one of the great literary masterpieces of world literature. (Merrill F. Unger)

Job is a great story and lesson; I want to quickly walk you through the book to make an important point.

The book of Job addresses the issue of why the righteous suffer.

Who was Job?

> *There was a man in the land of Uz, whose name was Job; and that man was blameless and upright, and one who feared God and shunned evil. And seven sons and three daughters were born to him. Also, his possessions were seven thousand sheep, three thousand camels, five hundred yoke of oxen, five hundred female donkeys, and a very large household, so that this man was the greatest of all the people of the East. (Job 1:1–3 NKJV)*

Job was a righteous and wealthy man who feared God. In chapter 1, verses 6–12, God and Satan are speaking about Job.

> *Now there was a day when the sons of God came to present themselves before the LORD, and Satan also came among them. And the LORD said to Satan, "From where do you come?"*
>
> *So, Satan answered the LORD and said, "From going to and fro on the earth, and from walking back and forth on it."*
>
> *Then the LORD said to Satan, "Have you considered My servant Job, that there is none like him on the earth, a blameless and upright man, one who fears God and shuns evil?"*
>
> *So, Satan answered the LORD and said, "Does Job fear God for nothing? Have You not made a hedge around him, around his household, and around all that he has on every side? You have blessed the work of his hands, and his possessions have increased in the land. But now, stretch out Your hand and touch all that*

> *he has, and he will surely curse You to our face!"*
>
> *And the LORD said to Satan, "Behold, all that he has is in your power; only do not lay a hand on his person."*
>
> *So, Satan went out from the presence of the LORD. (Job 1:6–12 NKJV)*

After receiving permission from God, Satan begins his assault on Job by killing his children and all but a few of his servants, and all his livestock were destroyed or stolen.

> *Now there was a day when his sons and daughters were eating and drinking wine in their oldest brother's house; and a messenger came to Job and said, "The oxen were plowing and the donkeys feeding beside them, when the Sabeans raided them and took them away—indeed they have killed the servants with the edge of the sword; and I alone have escaped to tell you!"*
>
> *While he was still speaking, another also came and said, "The fire of God fell from heaven and burned up the sheep and the servants and consumed them; and I alone have escaped to tell you!"*
>
> *While he was still speaking, another also came and said, "The Chaldeans formed three bands, raided the camels and took them away, yes, and killed the servants with the edge of the sword; and I alone have escaped to tell you!"*
>
> *While he was still speaking, another also came and said, "Your sons and daughters were eating and drinking wine in their oldest brother's house, and suddenly a great wind came from across the wilderness and struck*

> *the four corners of the house, and it fell on the young people, and they are dead; and I alone have escaped to tell you!"*
>
> *Then Job arose, tore his robe, and shaved his head; and he fell to the ground and worshiped. And he said: "Naked I came from my mother's womb, and naked shall I return there. The* Lord *gave, and the* Lord *has taken away; Blessed be the name of the* Lord*."*
>
> *In all this Job did not sin nor charge God with wrong. (Job 1:13–22 NKJV)*

Satan's assault did not cause Job to sin or curse God. Chapter 2 begins with another meeting of God and Satan.

> *Again, there was a day when the sons of God came to present themselves before the* Lord*, and Satan came also among them to present himself before the* Lord*. And the* Lord *said to Satan, "From where do you come?"*
>
> *Satan answered the* Lord *and said, "From going to and fro on the earth, and from walking back and forth on it."*
>
> *Then the* Lord *said to Satan, "Have you considered My servant Job, that there is none like him on the earth, a blameless and upright man, one who fears God and shuns evil? And still he holds fast to his integrity, although you incited Me against him, to destroy him without cause."*
>
> *So, Satan answered the* Lord *and said, "Skin for skin! Yes, all that a man has he will give for his life. But stretch out Your hand now, and touch his bone and his flesh, and he will surely curse You to Your face!"*

> *And the* Lord *said to Satan, "Behold, he is in your hand, but spare his life."*
>
> *So, Satan went out from the presence of the* Lord*, and struck Job with painful boils from the sole of his foot to the crown of his head. And he took for himself a potsherd with which to scrape himself while he sat in the midst of the ashes.*
>
> *Then his wife said to him, "Do you still hold fast to your integrity? Curse God and die!"*
>
> *But he said to her, "You speak as one of the foolish women speaks. Shall we indeed accept good from God, and shall we not accept adversity?"*
>
> *In all this Job did not sin with his lips. (Job 2:1–10 NKJV)*

Satan attacks Job's health, and even Job's wife says to him, "Curse God and die." Job maintains his integrity and does not curse God. Job's three friends—Eliphaz, Bildad, and Zophar—learn of Job's adversity and come to mourn with and comfort him. The four of them put dust on their heads and sat on the ground together for seven days and nights, not saying a word to him. It's hard to imagine how much pain he must have felt being covered in boils and losing all he had.

After seven days, Job began to speak, cursing the day that he was born. Then Job's friends started talking, each of the three giving his opinion on why all this misery befell on their friend Job. Eliphaz speaks first and proclaims that Job has sinned and is being chastened by God. Job defends himself and claims that his misery is not deserved and unjust.

Bildad speaks next and states that Job has sinned and should repent. Job again defends himself and rebukes Bildad, claiming to be righteous. Job then prays for a mediator, someone who can plead his case to God. Zopfar then speaks, urging Job to repent. Job then answers his critics, *"But you forgers of lies, you are all worthless physicians" (Job 13:4 NKJV).* This conversation carries on for twenty-seven chapters of the book. All the while, Job is praying, asking God why this has happened to him.

Elihu enters the story in chapter 32. Elihu is a young man that has been listening to the conversation of Job and his friends. Elihu contradicts Eliphaz, Bildad, and Zophar. He tells them that they are wrong to judge Job when they don't know the facts. Then Elihu condemns Job for his self-righteousness. He tells Job that only God is righteous and that He owes Job no explanation.

In the beginning of chapter 38, the Lord speaks to Job through a whirlwind. God chastises Job for questioning His silence. God tells Job that He is the creator and manager of the universe.

> *God asks Job, "Where were you when I laid the foundations of the earth? Tell Me if you have understanding. Who determined its measurements? Surely you know! Or who stretched the line upon it? To what were its foundations fastened? Or who laid its cornerstone." (Job 38:4–6 NKJV)*

> *Job, feeling humbled and ashamed responds to God, "Behold, I am vile; What shall I answer You? I lay my hand over my mouth. Once I have spoken, but I will not answer; Yes, twice, but I will proceed no further." (Job 40:4–5 NKJV)*

The LORD speaks to Eliphaz, Bildad, and Zophar.

> *And so it was, after the Lord had spoken these words to Job, that the Lord said to Eliphaz the Temanite, "My wrath is aroused against you and your two friends, for you have not spoken of Me what is right, as My servant*

Job has. Now therefore, take for yourselves seven bulls and seven rams, go to My servant Job, and offer up for yourselves a burnt offering; and My servant Job shall pray for you. For I will accept him, lest I deal with you according to your folly; because you have not spoken of Me what is right, as My servant Job has."

So Eliphaz the Temanite and Bildad the Shuhite and Zophar the Naamathite went and did as the LORD commanded them; for the LORD had accepted Job. And the LORD restored Job's losses when he prayed for his friends. Indeed, the LORD gave Job twice as much as he had before. Then all his brothers, all his sisters, and all those who had been his acquaintances before, came to him and ate food with him in his house; and they consoled him and comforted him for all the adversity that the LORD had brought upon him. Each one gave him a piece of silver and each a ring of gold.

Now the LORD blessed the latter days of Job more than his beginning; for he had fourteen thousand sheep, six thousand camels, one thousand yoke of oxen, and one thousand female donkeys. He also had seven sons and three daughters. And he called the name of the first Jemimah, the name of the second Keziah, and the name of the third Keren-Happuch. In all the land were found no women so beautiful as the daughters of Job; and their father gave them an inheritance among their brothers.

After this Job lived one hundred and forty years and saw his children and grandchildren for four generations. (Job 42:7–16 NKJV)

God redeems Job and doubles the livestock he had lost. God gave Job seven sons and three daughters. God did not double the number of children because they were not truly lost. Job is with the LORD now, and he has fourteen sons and six daughters.

I wanted to share this story with you because this could have been me or you instead of Job. Life can be like riding a roller coaster; the downs can be terrifying. When you feel like you are under attack, do as Job did—maintain your integrity and pray to God for help.

THE MIRACLE OF TONGUES

I have spent much time studying and researching this often-misunderstood topic. Hopefully I can provide clarification. Let us begin in Genesis 11, at the Tower of Babel. At that time, all the people of the world lived in one area and all spoke the same language. God divided the people into nations and scattered them over the earth. Each nation spoke its own unique language.

> *"Come, let Us go down and there confuse their language, that they may not understand one another's speech." So, the Lord scattered them abroad from there over the face of all the earth, and they ceased building the city. Therefore, its name is called Babel, because there the Lord confused the language of all the earth; and from there the LORD scattered them abroad over the face of all the earth. (Genesis 11:7–9 NKJV)*

After this, the nations of the world spoke languages unique to each nation, and the nations were geographically separate.

In the book of Acts chapter 2, on the day of Pentecost, the Holy Spirit comes from heaven and anoints the apostles, giving them the ability to speak in unlearned human languages so they could preach the Gospel to the nations in the language of each nation. On that day in Jerusalem, there were Jews present from at least fourteen different nations. Everyone there heard and understood the Gospel preached in his own nation's language.

> *When the Day of Pentecost had fully come, they were all with one accord in one place. And suddenly there came a sound from heaven, as of a rushing mighty wind, and it filled the whole house where they were sitting. Then there appeared to them divided tongues, as of fire, and one sat upon each of them. And they were all filled with the Holy Spirit and began to speak with other tongues, as the Spirit gave them utterance.*
>
> *And there were dwelling in Jerusalem Jews, devout men, from every nation under heaven. And when this sound occurred, the multitude came together, and were confused, because everyone heard them speak in his own language. Then they were all amazed and marveled, saying to one another, "Look, are not all these who speak Galileans? And how is it that we hear, each in our own language in which we were born? Parthians and Medes and Elamites, those dwelling in Mesopotamia, Judea and Cappadocia, Pontus and Asia, Phrygia and Pamphylia, Egypt and the parts of Libya adjoining Cyrene, visitors from Rome, both Jews and proselytes, Cretans and Arabs—we hear them speaking in our own tongues the wonderful works of God." So, they were all amazed and perplexed, saying to one another, "Whatever could this mean?" (Acts 2:1–12 NKJV)*

This was a miracle of God, a sign to be witnessed by the unbelieving Jewish people in Jerusalem on the day of Pentecost. The unbelieving Jews were those who had not recognized Yeshua (Jesus) as the Messiah. The ability to speak in tongues is a spiritual gift. The gifts of the Holy Spirit are unique skills and abilities given by the Holy Spirit to followers of Christ to serve God for the benefit of His people. Wisdom, knowledge, faith, and healing are other spiritual gifts. These gifts may be permanent or temporary.

The Holy Spirit decides what gift we are to have; we don't get to choose. Spiritual gifts are given to help others through love, not to edify oneself. The gift of tongues was the supernatural ability to speak in a human language they had never learned. This is known as the *unlearned human language view*. According to the Bible, the miraculous act of speaking in tongues took place three times in the book of Acts—chapters 2, 10, and 19.

> *For I say, through the grace given to me, to everyone who is among you, not to think of himself more highly than he ought to think, but to think soberly, as God has dealt to each one a measure of faith. For as we have many members in one body, but all the members do not have the same function, so we, being many, are one body in Christ, and individually members of one another. Having then gifts differing according to the grace that is given to us, let us use them: if prophecy, let us prophesy in proportion to our faith; or ministry, let us use it in our ministering; he who teaches, in teaching; he who exhorts, in exhortation; he who gives, with liberality; he who leads, with diligence; he who shows mercy, with cheerfulness. (Romans 12:3–8 NKJV)*

There are, however, churches that believe in speaking in tongues today. These are called *ecstatic utterances*. This is known as the *heavenly prayer language view*. This practice was common to all the pagan mystery religions with false gods. These ecstatic utterances are said to be in a language that only God knows; not even the speaker understands what he is saying. For instance, if a person was in a church of people and suddenly started praying out loud in a language that not even they understood, this would only be noise and a distraction.

This would in no way edify the church nor would be considered a miracle of God that would cause unbelievers to believe. Matthew 6:7 warns against babbling in prayer as the heathens do.

I strongly disagree with this belief. In fact, I have not found anything in Scripture to support this, nor have any of my teachers endorsed this belief. Also, *tongues* is a plural word referring to the many languages of the world. The language of heaven is one language. The main scripture that these questionable churches base their belief on is 1 Corinthians 14:2.

> *For he who speaks in a tongue does not speak to men but to God, for no one understands him; however, in the spirit he speaks mysteries. (1 Corinthians 14:2 NKJV)*

If we just read this single verse, it is easily misunderstood. But if we read the entire chapter, we see that Paul is saying something very different. Paul's message of the entire chapter 14 is about using our spiritual gifts to edify the church out of love. I notice in verse 2 that the word *tongue* is singular. Also, in verses 4, 9, 13, and 14, *tongue* is singular. I believe that Paul is referring to a single language that one might use in a personal prayer to the one God. When he uses the plural form, *tongues*, he is referring to one speaking to people (plural) of different nations. Paul's writings can be confusing at times.

In summary, the spiritual gift of speaking in tongues, as recorded in the book of Acts chapter 2, was a miracle of God. This took place in Jerusalem on the day of Pentecost, where a multitude of Jewish men from every nation were gathered. After witnessing the miracle of hearing the word of God in their own individual languages, many came to believe in Christ. About three thousand were baptized that day. In Acts chapter 10, at the house of Cornelius in Caesarea, Peter was preaching the word to a group of Gentiles. Many there accepted

Christ and were baptized. This was the first ever account of Gentiles believing in Christ and being baptized. In chapter 19, we read that Paul, in Ephesus, finds twelve men who had been baptized by John the Baptist but had not received the Holy Spirit at that time.

> *And when Paul had laid hands on them, the Holy Spirit came upon them, and they spoke with tongues and prophesied. (Acts 19:6 NKJV)*

These three accounts of speaking in tongues took place in the first century. This was a miracle of God, just as the miracles of Jesus were to be witnessed by unbelievers that they may believe and be saved. The miracle of the gift of tongues was in the speaking, not the hearing. I have talked with some people from the United Pentecostal Church. I've been told that they believe that one must speak in tongues to be saved and that everyone that was saved in the book of Acts spoke in tongues. I find no truth in this. The Bible tells us that we are saved by grace, faith in Jesus Christ, and the repentance of sin. Acts chapter 2 tells us that the three thousand that were saved at Pentecost, none that were saved that day, spoke in tongues.

THE GREATEST PROPHECY

The Bible is the greatest book ever written; there is no other book like it. The Bible covers roughly fifteen centuries and is written by forty human authors who were inspired by the living God. The Bible is a book of prophecy. There is no other book written that tells of events to come hundreds of years in the future with great accuracy. This is possible because the One who inspired the authors of the book is not bound by time and knows all. Through the omniscience of God, the Bible declares the end from the beginning.

There is a great prophecy in the book of Genesis that is overlooked by almost all. I've heard sermons, lectures, and Bible studies on Old Testament prophecy that have danced around this great truth but somehow missed this one. This is a prophecy of the end times that is recorded in the pages of Genesis. It is the prophetic story of Noah and the great flood.

In the Gospel of Matthew chapter 24 and in the Gospel of Luke chapter 17, Jesus speaks on the days of Noah.

> ***And as it was in the days of Noah, so it will be also in the days of the Son of Man: They ate, they drank, they married wives, they were given in marriage, until the day that Noah entered the ark, and the flood came and destroyed them all. (Luke 17:26–27 NKJV)***

In Genesis chapter 6, we find that God was grieved because the hearts of man had become wicked and evil.

> *Then the LORD saw that the wickedness of man was great in the earth, and that every intent of the thoughts of his heart was only evil continually. And the LORD was sorry that He had made man on the earth, and He was grieved in His heart. So, the LORD said, "I will destroy man whom I have created from the face of the earth, both man and beast, creeping thing and birds of the air, for I am sorry that I have made them." But Noah found grace in the eyes of the LORD. (Genesis 6:5–7 NKJV)*

It is estimated, at that time, there were one billion people on the earth; but God could find only one righteous man—Noah.

> *This is the genealogy of Noah. Noah was a just man, perfect in his generations. Noah walked with God. (Genesis 6:9 NKJV)*

God commands that Noah build an ark that would house him, his wife, their three sons and his sons' wives, a male and a female of each kind of animal, and seven of all clean animals. God told Noah that He would bring a great flood to destroy the world and all humans and all air-breathing animals, all except those on the ark. The construction of the great ark took 120 years. When it was completed, Noah and his family boarded the ark, and God called the chosen animals to the ark.

When they were all on board, God closed the door and sealed it. Then the rain came and covered the earth. It rained forty days and nights. The whole earth was submerged in water, and every air-breathing creature on the earth was no more, except those that God had saved. Noah, his family, and the animals were on the ark 371 days before the water had subsided enough for them to leave the ark. God then commanded Noah and his family to multiply and populate the earth. God promised to never destroy the earth again by water and put the rainbow in the sky as a symbol of His covenant with man. Yes, I left out many details, but my point is made.

God tells us in His Word that He will destroy the earth again but by fire (2 Peter 3:1–13). And again He will save the righteous to dwell with Him in His kingdom forever. God made a covenant with Noah to preserve him and all those on the ark (Genesis 6:14–18). God is offering a covenant to everyone that lives today—that, if we will believe in His Son, confess that He is Lord, and repent of our sins, we shall be saved. God loves us all more than we can comprehend. Come to the cross, give your life to the Lamb of God, and be saved.

> *For God so loved the world, that he gave his only begotten Son, that whosoever believeth in him should not perish, but have everlasting life. For God sent not his Son into the world to condemn the world; but that the world through him might be saved. (John 3:16–17 KJV)*

ADDITIONAL THOUGHTS

The Book of Life

God keeps a record of who is saved called the Book of Life. The book of Revelation tells us that all not found written in the Book of Life will be cast into the lake of fire.

> *And anyone not found written in the Book of Life was cast into the lake of fire. (Revelation 20:15 NKJV)*

I have always heard and believed that our names are written in the Book of Life at the time of salvation, when we accept Christ. A few years ago, I was having a conversation with one of my seminary professors on the topic of salvation. I asked him when our names are written in the Book of Life. He told me the Bible tells us that the Book of Life was written before the foundation of the world. Surprised by his response, I did some research and discovered that he is right. I will list the relevant scriptures at the end.

We must always remember that God is omniscient and He makes no mistakes. God has a plan that spans from before creation and beyond the end of the age, and He knows all that will happen in between. So God knew that I would accept Jesus and be saved thousands of years before I was born, and He knows everyone who will be saved. This, of course, includes the Old Testament people as well. They were saved by God the Father in those days because the Messiah had not yet come.

This is not predestination that the Calvinists believe. Every person has free will to choose to accept God and be saved or to deny

God and be condemned to hell. We still must make our decision even though God knew from the beginning how we would ultimately choose. In a way, we are predestined but by our own choosing. Therefore, the Bible uses the words like *the chosen* and *the elect.*

The more I learn and understand about God and His perfect plan, the more I am in awe of Him. He knew from the beginning who would choose Him and be saved and still lets us make all our decisions, good and bad. Every time someone gets saved, God is glorified. And for those who deny Him and will be cast into the lake of fire, God will be glorified because He offered them salvation but they rejected Him. The infinite intelligence of God is just amazing.

> *All who dwell on the earth will worship him, whose names have not been written in the Book of Life of the Lamb slain from the foundation of the world. (Revelation 13:8 NKJV)*

> *The beast that you saw was, and is not, and will ascend out of the bottomless pit and go to perdition. And those who dwell on the earth will marvel, whose names are not written in the Book of Life from the foundation of the world, when they see the beast that was, and is not, and yet is. (Revelation 17:8 NKJV)*

> *For whom He foreknew, He also predestined to be conformed to the image of His Son, that He might be the firstborn among many brethren. (Romans 8:29 NKJV)*

> *Just as He chose us in Him before the foundation of the world, that we should be holy and without blame before Him in love. (Ephesians 1:4 NKJV)*

The call of the Holy Spirit

We are now living in what is called the Church Age. The Church Age began on the day of Pentecost, when the Holy Spirit was sent by the Father to the apostles who were gathered in Jerusalem (Acts 2), and will end on the day of the Rapture, when God's people are "caught up" to heaven. This is the time that the Holy Spirit has been poured out on man to do His divine work.

One role of the Holy Spirit is to convict and call the lost. The Holy Spirit has the ability to consciously or unconsciously make unbelievers aware of the existence of God and realize that they are guilty of sin. All people are created in the image of God and, therefore, have a subconscious awareness of the existence of God. This awareness causes a conflict within the mind and heart of the unsaved person that can go on for years. The sinner must make a conscious decision—either to accept the calling of the Spirit and be saved through Christ or to rebuke the Spirit and continue in sin.

Many people attempt to put off making this decision. This procrastination is very dangerous. No one can be saved without the calling of the Holy Spirit. We do not know how much time we have left. Therefore, tomorrow may be too late. When you feel the Spirit convicting you, heed the call by praying the salvation prayer right then. Do not delay; you may not get another opportunity.

> *Now may the God of hope fill you with all joy and peace in believing, that you may abound in hope by the power of the Holy Spirit. (Romans 15:13 NKJV)*

> *This is He who came by water and blood—Jesus Christ, not only by water, but by water and blood. And it is the Spirit who bears witness because the Spirit is truth. (1 John 5:6 NKJV)*

> ***Behold, I stand at the door and knock. If anyone hears My voice and opens the door, I will come into him and dine with him, and he with Me. (Revelation 3:20 NKJV)***

The Holy Spirit has been working in His role in the Trinity from the beginning, unannounced. In the book of Acts, the Spirit is formally introduced and poured out in a new and greater New Testament ministry. This new ministry includes promoting the Gospel by calling and convicting the lost and indwelling believers at the time of salvation. In this New Testament ministry, the Holy Spirit's indwelling of a believer is permanent, or until we receive our glorified bodies. In the Old Testament role, the Spirit would indwell people for a temporary time, giving them supernatural abilities to perform certain tasks—for example, Samson in the book of Judges 14, 15, and 16; King Saul in 1 Samuel 16:14; and King David in Psalms 51:11.

Today, the moment a believer is saved, the Spirit indwells them and begins to plant spiritual gifts that will help them to do the will of God. Spiritual gifts may include wisdom, understanding, counsel, fortitude, knowledge, piety, and fear of the Lord. The Spirit will guide the believer toward righteousness and away from sin and danger. The Holy Spirit has come to exalt the Father and the Son, not Himself.

> ***But you shall receive power when the Holy Spirit has come upon you; and you shall be witnesses to Me in Jerusalem, and in all Judea and Samaria, and to the end of the earth. (Acts 1:8 NKJV)***

Prayer

Prayer is a conversation with God. Hearing God's part of the conversation takes time and patience. Prayers can be formal, on your knees and very reverent, or informal, while driving in an automobile.

There are many types of prayers. The salvation prayer is probably the most important prayer anyone will ever pray.

> Lord Jesus, I come to You now on my knees because I know that I am a sinner and that I need a Savior. I know that You died on the cross for me so that I can be saved and forgiven of my sins. Jesus, I want to commit my life to You because You gave Your life for me. I pray that You will accept me and help me to repent from my sinful life. I understand that my salvation is only possible through You and Your precious blood. I pray for Your will to be done in my life. I surrender all to You. Please come into my heart and live within me. It is in Your name that I pray. Amen.

Of course, you need to make it your own, in your own words. The salvation prayer is to Jesus because He is the Savior; He is the One that was crucified for us.

The Bible tells us to "pray without ceasing" (1 Thessalonians 5:17). God wants a close relationship with His people, and He wants us to talk to Him often. I personally have two formal prayers each day, one in the morning and the other in the evening, with several others throughout the day. During my formal prayers, I am alone on my knees—humble, sincere, and reverent. I want my prayer to glorify God.

> Almighty God, I come to you now to praise your Holy name, for who You are and for all You have done, and for all You are going to do. I praise You; for You are the Most High, El Elyon, the Great I Am, That I Am, Jehovah. You are the only God, and I will praise only Thee. Thank You, God, for all You have done for me. You have given me all I have, and You have always provided all I need. Thank You for your Son, who

> shed His blood for me and paid the price for my salvation. I confess my sins and ask You to forgive me. I pray that You will continue to watch over and protect me and my loved ones. I pray that my life will glorify and please You. In the name of Christ Jesus, I pray. Amen.

Let's talk about forgiveness and confession of sin. When we are saved, all our sins are forgiven—past, present, and future. When we go to the Lord in prayer, we are not so much asking for forgiveness of sin as we are confessing our sins. Confessing means that we are coming into agreement with God that we have done something wrong. This is important because, when we sin, we should experience a sense of guilt. Guilt tends to make us want to hide or separate from God, just as Adam and Eve hid from God in the garden (Genesis 3). Confessing our sins allows our relationship with God to be reconciled. We should then apologize to God for our sin and ask Him to help us to do better.

In my prayers, I like to start by praising God and acknowledging who He is. He is I Am, That I Am, YHWH. He is the only God. There is none other! I then give thanks for all that He has done, the creation, and for sending His only Son to die for me. I may have something at that time I want to give thanks for. I then will ask for His blessings and favor on me and my loved ones and maybe something else at that time. When I close my prayer, I say "In Jesus' name."

You might ask, "Why 'In Jesus' name'?" I'm glad you asked. During the life of Jesus, the Holy Temple in Jerusalem was the focal point of Jewish religious activities. The temple was the place of worship and sacrifice according to the law of Moses. Inside of the temple, there hung a great veil that separated the holy place from the holy of holies, where the spirit of God dwelt. This veil hung from the ceiling sixty feet to the floor. Only priests were allowed in the holy place that adjoined the holy of holies. Only the high priest was allowed to enter the holy of holies once a year on the Day of Atonement to sprinkle blood on the ark of the covenant as a sacrifice for the sins of the Jewish people.

At the moment that Jesus died on the cross, the veil was torn from top to bottom.

> *And Jesus cried out again with a loud voice and yielded up His spirit. Then, behold, the veil of the temple was torn in two from top to bottom; and the earth quaked, and the rocks were split. (Matthew 27:50–51 NKJV)*

When the veil was torn, this left the holy of holies open and exposed. This represents that God the Father was no longer there.

> *God, who made the world and everything in it, since He is Lord of heaven and earth, does not dwell in temples made with hands. (Acts 17:24 NKJV)*

Upon His death, the Lord Jesus Christ took the place of the veil that separated man from God. This gives man, Jew and Gentile, access to God the Father through Jesus.

> *Jesus said to him, "I am the way, the truth, and the life. No one comes to the father except through Me." (John 14:6 NKJV)*

When we pray, we pray to God the Father through His Son, Jesus.

What Bible version should we read?

This topic could make a book in itself. I will be brief as possible. I recommend the King James Bible because it is the purest version available today. Other common versions were translated from other Bibles that were flawed. The Latin Vulgate was full of intentional corruptions and mistranslations. Many versions today are influenced by the Vulgate. King James I of England appointed a team of forty-seven English scholars to translate the original Hebrew and Greek manuscripts so that they could write an accurate version of God's Holy Word. The King James Bible was completed in the year 1611.

I also recommend having a New King James Version on hand to help understand the Old English terminology. Many people lost their lives so that we may have a copy of God's Word; we should treasure ours.

Choosing the right church

Here in East Texas, there are literally churches on every corner, but how do we determine which is right for us? One of the best ways is to talk to friends and people that we associate with and ask why they attend or belong where they worship. I recommend visiting several churches in your area before deciding to become a member.

The church that you join needs to be doctrinally correct. The church's views on the Trinity and on believers' baptism should align with biblical teachings. The church should also be clear on the process of how we are to be saved—by grace, not by works, through the blood of Jesus Christ and nothing else. I believe that the Baptist doctrine is correct and consistent with the Bible. Most of the nondenominational churches in East Texas share this same view.

When you're visiting a church for the first time, I recommend that you introduce yourself and let it be known that you are visiting so that the members can make you feel welcome. In larger churches, it's easy to fall through the cracks. The church that I attend and many other churches have greeters by all the doors. They are there to welcome visitors and introduce them to the pastor and other members.

Keep in mind that we go to church to worship God, not to be entertained. Listen closely to the sermon. Is the pastor preaching the good news of the Gospel? After the service is over and you have left the church, take notice of how you feel inside. If you have a feeling of condemnation, visit another church. A worship service should give us a great sense of joy.

> ***For God did not send His Son into the world to condemn the world, but that the world through Him might be saved. (John 3:17 NKJV)***

Through the blood of Jesus, we can be saved and have everlasting life with Him in heaven. Knowing this should make our lives joyful.

Fasting

Biblical fasting is a sacrificial self-discipline of abstinence (usually of food) to gain a closer relationship with God. Fasting should be done in concert with prayer. Christians often fast when something troubling has entered their lives. They will fast and pray in hopes of gaining God's favor with a situation. Fasting can be private or public. This can be a group of believers praying and fasting in a union, asking for God's favor in a particular dilemma. For example, a pastor might ask the congregation to fast and pray for a church member that is going through heart surgery or something traumatic. Fasting can be very effective for gaining closeness and favor from God. I believe, when fasting privately, it is important to keep it between you and God. We should not tell people when we fast.

> ***Moreover, when you fast, do not be like the hypocrites, with a sad countenance. For they disfigure their faces that they may appear to men to be fasting. Assuredly, I say to you, they have their reward. (Matthew 6:16 NKJV)***

Some can't fast from food for health reasons but find other ways to fast. The principle of fasting is to give up something good or that one enjoys as a sacrifice to God. Some abstain from things like television, social media, or coffee for a time to spend time in prayer with God. For myself, I usually fast food from daylight until dark or for an entire twenty-four-hour period.

> ***So it was, when I heard these words, that I sat down and wept, and mourned for many days; I was fasting and praying before the God of heaven. (Nehemiah 1:4 NKJV)***

Tithing and offerings

The *tithe* literally means the tenth part. In the Old Testament, God commanded the children of Israel to give a tithe to the Levitical priests as payment for their work.

> ***Behold, I have given the children of Levi all the tithes in Israel as an inheritance in return for the work which they perform, the work of the tabernacle of meeting. (Numbers 18:21 NKJV)***

The Bible has a lot to say about tithings, offerings, and money. Jesus spoke about money frequently. Tithing was required in the Old Testament law. Many claim that Jesus set us free from the law, so we don't need to tithe anymore. That is true. However, we are still expected to give back to God for what we have received. How much have we received? Okay, let's talk about that. God created us and gave us our lives and everything we own, but He owns us and all our stuff. God pours out blessings on us daily and sent His Son to the cross to die for us so that we may enter His kingdom and live with Him forever. I personally can't put a value on that. Ten percent is an insignificant amount when I owe Him everything. Jesus said in Luke:

> ***Give, and it will be given to you: good measure, pressed down, shaken together, and running over will be put into your bosom. For***

> ***with the same measure that you use, it will be measured back to you. (Luke 6:38 NKJV)***

> *Now Jesus sat opposite the treasury and saw how the people put money into the treasury. And many who were rich put in much. Then one poor widow came and threw in two mites, which make a quadrans. So, He called His disciples to Himself and said to them,* ***"Assuredly, I say to you that this poor widow has put in more than all those who have given to the treasury; for they all put in out of their abundance, but she out of her poverty put in all that she had, her whole livelihood."*** *Mark (12:41–44 NKJV)*

I believe that how you give is important. God loves a cheerful giver. I want to recommend a great book that helped me on giving, *The Blessed Life* by Robert Morris. In Morris's book, he stresses that we are to give of our firstfruits. God doesn't want what we have left at the end of the month; He demands our first.

> *All the best of the oil, all the best of the new wine and the grain, their first fruits which they offer to the LORD, I have given them to you. (Numbers 18:12 NKJV)*

> *The first of the first fruits of your land you shall bring into the house of the LORD your God. You shall not boil a young goat in its mother's milk. (Exodus 23:19 NKJV)*

In his book, Morris states that he believes that God rebuked Cain's offering in Genesis 4 because Cain offered God some of his produce but not his first. Abel, however, offered God his firstborn of his flock.

> *And in the process of time it came to pass that Cain brought an offering of the fruit of the ground to the LORD. Abel also brought of the firstborn of his flock and of their fat. And the LORD respected Abel and his offering, but He did not respect Cain and his offering. And Cain was very angry, and his countenance fell. (Genesis 4:3–5 NKJV)*

This makes perfect sense to me. Most pastors that I have heard preach on this topic have said that God did not respect Cain's offering because it wasn't a blood-for-sin offering. This is the first-ever mention of an offering in the Bible, and there had been no reference to Cain sinning at that point.

Offerings are given in addition to the tithe to help others in need. If we don't give back, we are closing a door for His blessings on our lives.

> *Honor the LORD with your possessions, and with the first fruits of all your increase; So, your barns will be filled with plenty, and your vats will overflow with new wine. (Proverbs 3:9–10 NKJV)*

Sin unto death

What is sin unto death? Let's say there was a guy named Joe. Joe had been saved and baptized, but years later, we find him living a very sinful lifestyle. He is no longer going to church, and there is no repentance of his sin. If God sees that Joe has become a stumbling block to others (causing others to sin), God may call Joe home. This means that God may end Joe's physical life on earth and call him to heaven. There comes a point when God will no longer allow a believer to continue in unrepented sin. Remember, if we are saved, we cannot lose our salvation. Let's consider a scripture.

> *If anyone sees his brother sinning a sin which does not lead to death, he will ask, and He will give him life for those who commit sin not leading to death. There is sin leading to death. I do not say that he should pray about that. (1 John 5:16 NKJV)*

Here John is speaking to the church at Ephesus, but he is also speaking to all Christians. He is telling us to pray for our fellow Christians that we know committed a sin and that we should pray for them and ask forgiveness for their sin. I don't think that John is telling us not to pray for Joe because he is living a sinful lifestyle. I think that is not the point he is trying to make here. I believe that John is making a distinction between sin unto death and daily sin. I think we not only should be praying for Joe but should also go speak with him and pray with him. Other related scriptures on the subject include 1 Corinthians 11:28–32 and Hebrews 12:6.

Acts 5:1–10 tells us an account of sin unto death.

> *But a certain man named Ananias, with Sapphira his wife, sold a possession. And he kept back part of the proceeds, his wife also being aware of it, and brought a certain part and laid it at the apostles' feet. But Peter said, "Ananias, why has Satan filled your heart to lie to the Holy Spirit and keep back part of the price of the land for yourself? While it remained, was it not your own? And after it was sold, was it not in your own control? Why have you conceived this thing in your heart? You have not lied to men but to God." Then Ananias, hearing these words, fell down and breathed his last. So great fear came upon all*

> *those who heard these things. And the young men arose and wrapped him up, carried him out, and buried him. Now it was about three hours later when his wife came in, not knowing what had happened. And Peter answered her, "Tell me whether you sold the land for so much?" She said, "Yes, for so much." Then Peter said to her, "How is it that you have agreed together to test the Spirit of the Lord? Look, the feet of those who have buried your husband are at the door, and they will carry you out." Then immediately she fell down at his feet and breathed her last. And the young men came in and found her dead, and carrying her out, buried her by her husband. (Acts 5:1–10 NKJV)*

The unpardonable sin

The Bible tells us that there is an unforgivable sin.

> ***But he who blasphemes against the Holy Spirit never has forgiveness, but is subject to eternal condemnation. (Mark 3:29 NKJV)***

My definition of *blasphemy* is irreverence or slander toward God either by words or actions. Remember, the Holy Spirit is God. However, the apostle Paul tells us that even this is forgivable.

> *And I thank Christ Jesus our Lord who has enabled me, because He counted me faithful, putting me into the ministry, although I was formerly a blasphemer, a persecutor, and an insolent man; but I obtained mercy because I did it ignorantly in unbelief. And the grace of our Lord was exceedingly abundant, with*

> *faith and love which are in Christ Jesus. This is a faithful saying and worthy of all acceptance, that Christ Jesus came into the world to save sinners, of whom I am chief. However, for this reason I obtained mercy, that in me first Jesus Christ might show all longsuffering, as a pattern to those who are going to believe on Him for everlasting life. (1 Timothy 1:12–16 NKJV)*

In the world we live today, the only unpardonable sin is by rejecting Jesus, by rejecting the call of the Holy Spirit. If a person dies never heeding the call of the Spirit, that person shall be condemned.

Time

I have a theory about time that I want to share with you; again this is my opinion. As I wrote earlier, in Genesis 1:1, "In the beginning God created the heavens and the earth," God creates time, space, and matter. Time did not exist until God created it. Our human minds struggle to comprehend this because it is difficult to imagine life without time. God created all that is, and all that He created is bound by time. However, God is not bound by time, space, or matter. He exists in the present, in the infinite future, and in the infinite past. It is God's will that heaven and earth be bound by time. The Bible tells us that all this will pass away.

> ***Heaven and earth will pass away, but My words will by no means pass away. (Matthew 24:35 NKJV)***

Our basic unit for measuring time is the day or a complete rotation of the earth. In ancient times, man measured a day by a cycle of daylight and of darkness—one day.

> *God called the light Day, and the darkness He called Night. So, the evening and the morning were the first day. (Genesis 1:5 NKJV)*

Now let's examine some scriptures from the book of Revelation.

> *Now I saw a new heaven and a new earth, for the first heaven and the first earth had passed away. Also, there was no more sea. (Revelation 21:1 NKJV)*

> *And God will wipe away every tear from their eyes; there shall be no more death, nor sorrow, nor crying. There shall be no more pain, for the former things have passed away. (Revelation 21:4 NKJV)*

> *The city had no need of the sun or of the moon to shine in it, for the glory of God illuminated it. The Lamb is its light. (Revelation 21:23 NKJV)*

> *Its gates shall not be shut at all by day (there shall be no night there). (Revelation 21:25 NKJV)*

> *There shall be no night there: They need no lamp nor light of the sun, for the Lord God gives them light. And they shall reign forever and ever. (Revelation 22:5 NKJV)*

In Revelation 21:1, we read that the first heaven and earth have passed away. In Revelation 21:4, we read there will be no death, sorrow, crying, or pain; for they have passed away. Revelation 21:23,25 and 22:5 tell us that there will be no day or night as we now have. For the glory of God and the Lamb will be the light, "and they shall reign forever and ever".

These five verses of Revelation are describing what life will be like in the New Jerusalem, or heaven. We can read and understand that there will be no darkness or nights. Therefore, there will be no days, as we now use to measure time. In Revelation 22:5, we read the words *them* and *they*, which are referring to all who are in the New Jerusalem, all who have been saved, the bride of Christ.

Taking all this into consideration, I believe that God created time as a controlling element over all His creation. All that God has created, the heaven and the earth and all that is on the earth, have a physical life limit. I believe that God started a proverbial clock in Genesis 1:1; and this clock will run until all the saints are home in the New Jerusalem, at which time God will stop the clock, ending time, and we shall reign with Him forever and ever. Amen.

On the topic of time, a few weeks ago, my Sunday school teacher Tommy told our class this story.

There were three apprentice demons that were being sent into the world to complete their apprenticeship. They were talking to Satan about their plans to tempt and ruin men.

The first demon said, "I will tell them there is no God".

Satan said, "That will delude not many, for they know there is a God".

Another demon said, "I will tell them there is no hell".

Satan answered, "You will deceive no one. Men know there is a hell."

The third demon said, "I will whisper into the ears of men and say, 'There is no hurry'".

"Go," said Satan. "You will ruin them by the thousands".

The most dangerous of delusions is that there is plenty of time.

> *He who testifies to these things says, **"Surely I am coming quickly."** Amen. Even so, come, Lord Jesus! The grace of our Lord Jesus Christ be with you all. Amen. (Revelation 22:20 NKJV)*

CONCLUSION

I hope these words have spoken to your soul and touched your heart. Whether you are not yet saved, are a new Christian, or have been a follower of Christ for years, the Bible's message is the same. God loves you and wants a relationship with you. To the unsaved, when you feel the call of the Holy Spirit, do not hesitate to respond. If you are alone, get on your knees and pray a salvation prayer and follow up with a pastor or a Christian friend as soon as possible.

I hope you feel like you know more about God than when you started reading this book. I ask again, If someone were to ask you who God is, what would your response be? I think that it is very important that every Christian be able to verbalize a response to that all-important question. We should always be prepared to defend our faith.

> *But sanctify the Lord God in your hearts, and always be ready to give a defense to everyone who asks you a reason for the hope that is in you, with meekness and fear. (1 Peter 3:15 NKJV)*

> *Holding fast the faithful word as he has been taught, that he may be able, by sound doctrine, both to exhort and convict those who contradict. (Titus 1:9 NKJV)*

Now that you have read this book, you have everything you need to carry out the Great Commission. In the Gospel of Matthew chapter 28, Jesus commands His disciples to "go therefore and make disciples."

> *And Jesus came and spoke to them, saying, "All authority has been given to Me in heaven and on earth. Go therefore and make disciples of all the nations, baptizing them in the name of the Father and of the Son and of the Holy Spirit, teaching them to observe all things that I have commanded you; and lo, I am with you always, even to the end of the age." Amen. (Matthew 28:18–20 NKJV)*

Now go forth and preach the Gospel of the Lord Jesus Christ.
For God has called us to be the light, and in
the light, darkness has no power.
I will be praying for God's blessings and mercy on you all.

—Matthew

ABOUT THE AUTHOR

As Matthew G. Morton wrote in the introduction of this book, his goal is to glorify God by helping others learn and understand more about God and His perfect plan of salvation for everyone. Matthew does not want it to be about him; however, he understands that readers will want to know something about the author.

Matthew was born and raised in Henderson, Texas, and has two children and two grandchildren. His career was with the Goodyear Tire and Rubber Company and is now retired.

Matthew was raised in the Methodist church; however, he joined a Baptist church and was baptized in 1992. He is currently an active member of First Baptist Church, where he serves in several ministries. Matthew has a brief story of how God called him to formal Bible education.

Matthew is an avid cyclist and was out for a ride one evening in August a few years ago. He was riding on a farm-to-market road, several miles from town, when his tire blew out. This was surprising to him because he had just recently replaced his tires and tubes. Even more surprising, as soon as this happened, a man in a brand-new pickup stopped and asked him if he needed help. Matthew says that he has had flats in the past, but no one has ever offered to help him. He asked the man if he would mind giving him a ride back into town, and he said "sure." Matthew loaded his bike and got in the man's truck but felt embarrassed because he was sweating on the man's nice seat.

On the way back to town, they were talking; the man said that his name was Steve and that he was the dean at Texas Baptist Institute (a small seminary in Henderson). Matthew began asking about the school and got information on programs that were offered there. Later that night, Matthew felt that God was calling him to that school. The next week, Matthew enrolled and began classes. He wasn't sure exactly what God wanted him to accomplish there but was willing to be obedient to God's calling. After two years of classes there, a friend recommended that Matthew consider enrolling at Faith Bible Institute in Monroe, LA. After researching the school online, he immediately enrolled and began a three-year program and will graduate in 2024.

Printed in the USA
CPSIA information can be obtained
at www.ICGtesting.com
LVHW070233181023
761432LV00016B/375